W9-BWI-590

LIBERATING CREATION

LIBERATING CREATION

Foundations of Religious Social Ethics

GIBSON WINTER

BJ
1251
.W56
1981

ST. JOSEPH'S UNIVERSITY STX
BJ1251.W56 1981
Liberating creation :

CROSSROAD • NEW YORK

204632

1981
The Crossroad Publishing Company
575 Lexington Avenue, New York, NY 10022

Copyright © 1981 by Gibson Winter

All rights reserved. No part of this book may be reproduced, stored in a retrieval system, or transmitted, in any form or by any means, electronic, mechanical, photocopying, recording, or otherwise, without the written permission of The Crossroad Publishing Company.

Printed in the United States of America

Library of Congress Cataloging in Publication Data

Winter, Gibson.
Liberating creation.

Bibliography: p. 135
Includes index.
1. Christian ethics—Anglican authors. 2. Social ethics. 3. Technology and ethics. I. Title.
BJ1251.W56 261 81-5364
ISBN 0-8245-0032-6 AACR2

With gratitude to colleagues and students who helped to forge this work

CONTENTS

INTRODUCTION

THE twentieth century is heir to deadly perils growing out of industrial and technological development. Mineral and fossil resources stored up for billions of years are approaching exhaustion. A biosphere that preserved life over eons is endangered. Many forms of life are being speeded toward extinction. Even the human species, author of this project, begins to appear fragile as its tools threaten it with annihilation. Hence, radical questions are being raised about the future of technological society; the whole direction of this Western project is now in doubt.

Wrestling with such foundational questions is the foolishness to which religious ethicists are called: foolishness because there is no panacea for human ills; a calling because the human is a religious and moral species, destined for freedom and responsibility. There is, to be sure, no general agreement on what discipline, if any, can deal with such radical questions. Theology would have pursued these matters a few centuries ago. Philosophy undertook such inquiries in the classical period. The human sciences bravely faced such questions in the wake of the Enlightenment. Today, the humanistic and historical disciplines are so fragmented that no single field claims competence for such questions. Somewhat like the biological sciences confronted with environmental threats for which their specializations were inappropriate, the religio-moral disciplines require an integrative or interdisciplinary approach to the crisis of our age. In principle, theology or religious studies or religious social ethics or human science could provide the integrative center for such a task.

Unfortunately, the methods of inquiry that control these disciplines focus attention on micro-problems and away from the encompassing issues of this age. In an age of incoherence, religio-moral inquiries are challenged to seek coherence. This is the aim of the present inquiry. It could as well be called theology or religious social ethics or human science so long as the subject matter, human dwelling, is understood to include practical, moral, and religious issues.

What, then, are the radical questions confronting the technological age? To anticipate the inquiry, some of those questions can be identified, bearing in mind that the questions shape the answers, so that the questions have to be subject to revision.

Power is a central problem of the technological age. From its inception, this age has been marked by a search for power over its world. To this extent, Francis Bacon was its prophet if not its mentor. The passion for mastery led to advances in science, exploration of distant lands, conquest and enslavement of peoples throughout the globe, and development of techniques for mass production and distribution of goods. The struggle for mastery pitted the strong against the weak, generating disparities of rich and poor, conflicts between metropolitan centers of power and dependent satellites. Thus, distributive justice became an intractable problem for a technologized world. Those who control capital and technology dominate the earth. Moreover, inequality in the distribution of power and wealth is entangled with the question of the purpose of this technological project.

To what end or purpose is the world engaged in this insatiable drive for domination? So long as that passion consumes the age, radical disparities of power and wealth will plague the earth. The aim of the technological age is seldom questioned, since it is taken for granted that peoples everywhere should scramble for all the power and wealth they can command. When the question is raised, the answer seems obvious: human mastery should lead to the good society, empowering and protecting the human species. Since this is not in fact the case, that glib answer proves to be irrelevant. Peoples are hungry on this earth who never knew want in the past (Fallers). Each step in the pursuit of mastery brings the human species closer to annihilation. How then is one to understand the purpose of this technological project? Unless the question of the meaning of the human project is confronted, there can be no escape from the domination and injustice that follow upon the drive for mastery. Only a fundamental transformation can halt the slide into oblivion.

Difficulties attend the raising of foundational questions. It is impossible to step out of the world into an observation booth and contemplate the course of events. Questioning the purpose of one's age includes the questioner. The technical thinking that dominates the age also disfigures the questioning, reducing every issue to a matter of technical skill or factual knowledge. Ecological questions are reduced to better management of the environment. Questions of urban poverty are answered with bureaucratic programs which employ more middle-class people. The violence in marginalized communities of urban and rural areas is countered with programs of "legalized" suppression. The technological age subverts its own questioning by its commitment to technical answers. Technical domination of thought leads to the evasion of fundamental questions. This is the challenge facing any discipline that is so rash as to raise radical questions about the methods and aims of the technical project.

Rethinking the direction of a particular epoch is only possible when contradictions disrupt normal expectations. Such dislocations lead to paradigm shifts, transformations in the root metaphors which furnish clues to the encompassing world. This is the ground on which an alternative perspective on the technological age can be raised. History has appropriate times for questions and the changes that follow in their wake. This seems to be such a time. The mechanistic paradigm is proving self-destructive. Some of the contradictions that plague the technical project have already been noted. Many more could be delineated. Doubts about this age have actually been voiced from different quarters for a century or more. Some of the challenges came from a nostalgia for the past, sounding a return to a hierarchical, organic order of life that was passing. Other criticisms came from those who yearned for hierarchy but intended to impose it through collective domination. The romantics made important protests but failed to touch the mechanistic age at its center. The collectivists simply adopted the violence of the technical order on behalf of an outmoded hierarchy of blood and soil. This battle between mechanistic and organicist perspectives pitted Enlightenment against ancient legacies of order. In different forms, this struggle has plagued the twentieth century. Meanwhile, a creative paradigm of dwelling is taking hold in various fields of thought and action, gradually displacing the megamachine and its ancient foe, collectivistic hierarchy. This new paradigm is rooted in the artistic powers of the human species. It combines the creative capacities that empowered the technical project and the participatory roots that generated the organicist heritage.

Artistic way of being is an original dynamic in human evolution. Tools, language, decoration, ritual, games, and myths disclose these artistic powers. Perhaps this artistry was so close to the very being of the human species that it never gained ascendancy over other paradigms. Root metaphors or paradigms seem to emerge from a people's experience of its world—its gardening, gathering, hunting, reproduction, dwelling under the sky and on the earth. Organicist hierarchies of various sorts have held sway over human life for ages and ages, only gradually being displaced by mechanism in recent centuries. Artistic process, rooted in ancient human practice, is only now gaining ascendancy as a paradigm of human dwelling. Chapter I below traces the clash of paradigms and the emergence of this artistic metaphor.

Investigation of the purpose of a human world turns on the question of what constitutes dwelling. The mechanistic paradigm has placed almost insuperable roadblocks before such inquiries. Mechanistic thought and action reduce work, politics, marriage, and education to a technical, means-end process which flattens the world, suppressing the symbols and rituals that found and orient human life. This eclipse of symbols has often been remarked by critics of the technological age. The cliché for this repression is the idea of secularization. The modern world is presumed to be secularized, living and working by its calculations. However, the secularization thesis is an ideology that conceals the life commitments of the technological age. Critique of this ideology involves a reconsideration of the foundational role of symbols in human dwelling. Chapter 2 traces the symbolic order to the poetic creativity of the human species. The hierophany of the sacred in symbolization is an artistic event of receptivity and creativity. Within this perspective, one recognizes that the human species dwells symbolically on the earth.

The recognition that dwelling is an artistic process reveals another important dimension of social process. Dwelling is a lived interpretation of the symbolized world. Technological organization is a way of inscribing the symbolized world of work in systems of management and control. Scientific investigations are ways of deciphering the coding of a symbolized nature. Even human dispositions toward the natural realm are inscriptions of a symbolic orientation in attitudes and interests. Since lived interpretation is essentially a linguistic process, the artistic paradigm unfolds the creative powers of metaphor in such inscriptions. History can then be understood as the reciprocal interplay of symbolizations and interpretations as they shift over time.

Reflective interpretations of the world in philosophy, theology, and the human sciences are grounded in lived interpretations and oriented by the symbols that found them. In interpreting human history and dwelling, Paul Ricoeur's study of the written text proves helpful. Within an artistic paradigm, dwelling is an analogue to the written text. To interpret human dwelling is to read the societal text. Ricoeur's proposal that the text can be read in a threefold structure of guess, explanation, and comprehension thus furnishes a method for social interpretation. *Guess* refers to the informing perspective that guides the reading of the text. In the present inquiry, the artistic paradigm is a guiding perspective or guess. The *explanatory* power of this guess is traced through the founding of dwelling in the hierophany of symbols and the unfolding of that symbolic world in lived interpretations. The moment of *comprehension,* disclosing the world that is projected in the text, is explicated in chapter 3, where the theological vision of artistic process is developed.

Chapter 4 sets forth an artistic interpretation of the religious heritage of the West. The vision relies upon the work of Paul Klee. It is a vision of a good creation, a foundational symbol of the biblical heritage. Divine and human powers collaborate in the cocreation of a world of justice and peace. The disruptive forces of pride and domination become structured in lived interpretations but do not hold the final word in creation. The truth and falsity of the technological project come to light against this symbolic background. Appropriate ordering of the mechanistic and organicist paradigms also follows from this vision of creation. To this extent, an artistic vision transcends the nemesis of mechanism and the collectivism of organic hierarchy. (For those whose orientation is primarily practical, this chapter might well be read first.)

These reflections were generated by the injustice of life in a technological age. They point toward a transformative praxis, a direction toward justice and the survival of the human species. In this respect, religious social ethics is the reflective work of all peoples as they struggle to throw off forces of domination and gain responsibility for their lives. This is the praxis of liberation to which reflection can make a limited but useful contribution. This is the threshold of faith and transformative action which is the aim of a religious social ethic.

1

METAPHOR AND SOCIETY

In a slightly sardonic yet serious article, Paul Bohannan puzzled about the depressing effect of certain birthdays in American culture (Bohannan: 28). He himself found thirty-one years a particularly troubling occasion: he had been officially an adult for ten years, had been caught up in a war, and to all intents and purposes had accomplished little. For others sixty or sixty-five (retirement), or for some women forty-five (children leaving, life changing) become critical times. Bohannan contrasted this Western experience of time and age, calculated in numbers on base 10, with the life of the Tiv in Nigeria whom he had studied. As he observes, a Tiv child ceases to be a "lap child" when the youngster walks, becoming then a "small child." He notes, "Among Tiv, to get old is 'to finish one's body.' " How many parents in contemporary Western society fuss and worry over *when* a child walks, talks, gets baby teeth, learns to read and count, etc.? How much of life in this highly technologized society is calculated rather by years of work, annuities, retirement dates, eligibility for military service, weeks of unemployment insurance or years of accumulated pension credits? Paul Bohannan makes a simple point in his article: we get into trouble with certain segments in time because we operate in our culture on base 10. The striking thing about our lives in contrast to older cultures is that we operate on a linear, mathematical time line that often has little to do with personal or biological rhythms. We measure on linear scales what can only be measured in terms of a space-time that grows and unfolds.

As they have become familiar with patterns of life in traditional societies during recent centuries, Western people have assumed that the calculative thinking and organizing in their societies reflect "rational" or fully human development. On this evolutionary time line, traditional peoples were thought of as ignorant and confused, living in a world of fantasy which modern Western society has now left behind through its achievements in science and technology. The world of sacred and biological rhythms could be dismissed as a world of superstition that represented humanity's infantile period. Although the matter is seldom stated so crassly, this has certainly been the implicit understanding of Western peoples, an understanding that was imposed on traditional peoples as they were dominated, exploited, and in some cases exterminated by the expansion of the West. Underlying this clash of Western technological and traditional worlds is a radically different imagery of the world. Traditional peoples, and most of the older, higher civilizations, operate with some variant of a biological or organicist imagery of life and cosmos. They live in a world of more-than-human powers, ordered according to the rhythms of biological or organic growth and decay. Even Platonic and Aristotelian thought, whatever their differences, presupposed an organicist process on which human understanding could be modeled (Cornford: 47–95; Barker: 218–31, 276–80). If one is careful not to project an unwarranted homogeneity on these various peoples and cultures, it can be safely argued that a common source of imagery provides coherence in their worlds. This source is the biological and organic process which is closest to them and directly implicated in their methods of production and survival.[1]

The calculative, linear imagery that lends coherence to the modern technological world is not necessarily better or more rational than that of traditional peoples. It is simply different. It has proved useful in organizing mass production, assembly lines, large areas of coordinated activity, systematic planning of transportation, communication, marketing, and military power. It has proved damaging to the natural environments of earth, air, water, and communal space.[2] It has proved inimical to the intimate communities of personal, familial, and neighborhood life.[3] It has also imposed serious restrictions on the creative capacities of persons and peoples, for survival in such a mechanistic world requires conformity to highly routinized and repetitive patterns of work and life. This is not to deny the enhancement of power that the linear, mechanistic image has brought to the modern world, albeit power that is necessarily concentrated in the organizers of the process. However, the differences between industrialized and traditional peoples cannot be reduced to the linear terms of a mechanistic mind, treating the modern as adult and the traditional as infantile. It is rather a fundamental difference between a world organized around the rhythms of life and nature versus a world organized by systems of calculation (Heidegger, 1977: 169–73).

It would be easy to exaggerate the differences between traditional and modern imagery. There is considerable evidence that archaic peoples employed many of the techniques and rules of thumb which enabled them to calculate and build what they needed. Gardening, raising stock, and building canoes require technical skill and knowledge that are comparable to our own (Malinowski: chap. 4). By the same token, modern peoples also organize aspects of their lives around more personal and natural rhythms, thus achieving some relief from the mechanized systems that control them. The weekend, the holiday, family reunions and evenings for gathering are detached from the mechanistic process that governs so much of technological life.

The clash of traditional, organicist imagery and mechanistic orientation is reflected in the controversy over sexism in industrialized societies. The technological world emerged in a period of male domination. Men controlled the industries, governments, commerce, banking, and exploration during the centuries of industrialization. Capitalistic industry was largely a masculine enterprise at the top, although women served as a labor force in the reproductive process at home and often in the factories and shops. The metaphoric imagery of the machine undergirded this industrial and technical development (Mumford: chap. 3). However, the organicist metaphor of biological organization continued to shape the understanding of marriage, the place of women, and the authority of the husband and father. Women were viewed as lesser beings, meant for servile roles under the authority of men. The rationalization of this organicist hierarchy of male superiority was rooted in classical metaphysics which treated the feminine as matter to be formed and informed by the masculine power (Ruether). In this way, the technologized societies of the West have lived in two worlds. The industries, bureaucracies, and transnational corporate structures are organized as systems of manipulation and control. They continue to be dominated by men, often imposing masculine patterns of conduct on the women who are able to gain access to these positions of power. Meanwhile, an organicist, hierarchical network of metaphoric images shapes the patterns of family life, feminine styles of dress, employment of women as sexual objects for advertising, and the imposition of lower pay scales on women in the work force.

The struggle over sexist discrimination is, to be sure, much more complicated than a clash of metaphoric networks of interpretation. However, the conflict of organicist and mechanistic modes of orientation runs through many of the misunderstandings in this oppressive situation. Movements like Right to Life and Moral Majority are trying to force women back into servitude in kitchen and home. Their understanding of women is biologically defined in organicist imagery. At the same time, there is some truth in their concern for home and family. Mechanistic orientations undercut many of the intimate ties that bind persons, families, and communities together. So the clash of these root metaphors or worlds reflects distortions in both images of human community, mechanistic and organicist.

The shape of the struggle over sexism becomes clearer when it is viewed as a clash of root metaphors. Human beings are understanding beings. They dwell in the world through thoughts and feelings that are mediated by language and symbols. In the human world, trees are not just bundles of energy in particular shapes. Trees are interpreted events, full of associations, textures, and meanings. So it is with every aspect of human life and activity. The human species abides in its world through the meanings borne in thought and discourse. This is not to suggest that the world is merely a mental phenomenon, for by the way people treat things and others, by the way they organize work and family life, people express their understandings and feelings. At the same time, ways of working, acting, loving, and fearing shape ways of understanding and interpreting. To this extent, the comprehensive metaphors that give clues to the coherence of things serve to shape human activities even as they are reshaped by patterns of life and work. The mechanistic metaphor emerged slowly in the West. As mechanism shaped science and technique, capitalistic organization and political systems, it became a dominant mode of interpretation of nature, life, and cosmos. Even the medical profession gradually came to understand the human organism as a machine, developing technologized medicine around this imagery.

Sexist oppression cannot be overcome simply by straightening out the clash of metaphors anymore than the conflict of traditional and industrialized societies can be resolved by proper metaphoric interpretation. These oppressions and conflicts are generated by the politico-economic institutions of modern society. Furthermore, the symbol systems of traditional and industrialized societies are in a life and death struggle. The symbolisms of land and community, nature and life, people and nation, are irreconcilably at odds between older, organicist communities and what Lewis Mumford has vividly designated the "megamachine." This struggle points to a symbolism of dwelling that reaches beyond organicism and mechanism. The same holds for the symbolization of women in the technologized societies. The Women's Movement is uncovering a symbolism of men and women that founds a sense of the human being who may be masculine or feminine. This symbolism is at odds with both organicist and mechanistic symbolism. However, root metaphors furnish important clues to the institutional struggles and symbolic clashes. This is a war of worlds, for it is a contention between total views of life and foundational symbolizations of the world. Root metaphors furnish important clues to such totalities. In fact, it is only through such clues that one can gain a sense of the coherence of the total world that encompasses thought and life. There is no way to subsume one's total world under a concept. Only a comprehensive metaphor can guide thought toward that totality. In this sense, the root metaphor is the first step toward foundational understanding.

ROOT METAPHORS

Considerable attention has been given in recent years to comprehensive or root metaphors. Stephen Pepper explored four such metaphors in sorting out different approaches to method in philosophy. He found that formism, organicism, mechanism, and contextualism had been the dominant metaphors in Western, philosophic thought (Pepper: 146). His pioneering work in this field has significant, if indirect, bearing on the subject of this book. He was exploring the crucial place of metaphor. However, I am arguing further that certain metaphoric networks become dominant in a total society, shaping modes of thought, action, decision, and life.

Robert Nisbet in his study *Social Change and History* traced the emergence and transformations in the organicist metaphor in Western thought. Despite his tendency to stress the continuity of this metaphor in the West, Nisbet's study is a striking confirmation of the power of metaphor in organizing thought and experience. Contrary to Nisbet's thesis, however, I shall argue that organicism was displaced as a dominant metaphor in the West by mechanism.[4] The rise of a technologized science in the modern period gradually led to the displacement of organicist imagery. Nevertheless, organicism has continued to play an important part in Western life, particularly, as noted above, in the more personal spheres of family and religious life. But this displacement accounts for the radical incoherences in personal and organizational life that characterize modern society. The important point is that comprehensive, metaphoric networks do inform thought and life.

To understand more fully this informative role, it will be necessary to examine briefly some recent studies on the nature of metaphor. Philip Wheelwright's investigations highlight the fundamental role of metaphor in language. He draws on poet

Wallace Stevens's reference to "the symbolic language of metamorphosis," asserting:

> What really matters in a metaphor is the psychic depth at which things of the world, whether actual or fancied, are transmuted by the cool heat of imagination. The transmutative process that is involved may be described as *semantic motion;* the idea of which is implicit in the very word "metaphor," since the motion (*phora*) that the word connotes is a semantic motion—the double imaginative act of outreaching and combining that essentially marks the metaphoric process. [Wheelwright, 1962: 71f.]

This simultaneous extension by likeness and juxtaposition of the different in one metaphoric statement ("my salad days when I was green in judgment") yields the metaphoric event. Wheelwright stresses the tensive, innovative power of metaphor in this event, the release of semantic energy through a tensive fusion of terms.

Paul Ricoeur has elaborated this notion of tensive metaphor as it occurs in the sentence. He proposes that the tension in the metaphor is generated by two opposed interpretations in an utterance. The conflict of these two interpretations (literal and figurative) sustains the metaphor. In this sense resemblance plays its role in metaphor by establishing a "kinship where ordinary vision does not perceive any relationship" (Ricoeur, 1976: 51). Ricoeur subordinates the notion of substitution metaphors, where a figurative term is substituted for a literal meaning, to the tensive, predicative metaphor that discloses something new. He argues that metaphors are predicative and belong fundamentally to the sentence. Semantic innovation occurs in the metaphoric event through the attribution of an unusual or unexpected predicate. Two conclusions follow from Ricoeur's interpretation of metaphoric utterances. (1) There is no way to translate a metaphoric utterance into other terms, for a tension metaphor creates its meaning and is not reducible. (2) A metaphoric utterance "has more than emotive value because it offers new information. A metaphor, in short, tells us something new about reality" (Ricoeur, 1976: 52f.). Metaphoric utterance is, then, a creative mode of knowledge. As Robert Nisbet put it,

"Metaphor is a way of knowing—one of the oldest, most deeply embedded, even indispensable ways of knowing in the history of human consciousness" (Nisbet: 4). Thus, if one assumes that comprehensive metaphors furnish coherence in a people's world, there is no way to reduce such metaphors to rational formulae or systems of thought. A people may shift its organizing metaphor over time, but it cannot dispense with a comprehensive metaphor without losing a sense of coherence.

To make the matter immediate, these reflections are themselves developing in a metaphoric framework, in this case that of an artistic metaphor—the reasons for choosing this framework shall be taken up shortly. But briefly, I contend that it is metaphoric imagery rather than mere fact or transcendent idea which gives the clue to the archetypal energies that generate the world of meaning.[5] Metaphor and the poetic genre are of the essence of artistic process; hence, to turn to metaphor is already to reflect in artistic terms. A further broad consideration is that metaphors are ways of knowing; hence, comprehensive metaphors give understanding of the world. Moreover, particular metaphors organize knowledge in particular ways. Different metaphors present different worlds. A shift in metaphors, then, may mean new insights into the nature of life and new possibilities of human dwelling. If the present age faces a crisis of root metaphors, a shift in metaphors may open new vistas of human possibilities. Metaphor is, in this sense, a vehicle of transcendence and freedom.

Paul Ricoeur has taken a further step in studying metaphors which has direct bearing on another integrative element in human society, the symbol. He was led to the study of metaphor when a direct approach to symbol seemed inadequate (Ricoeur, 1976: 45f.). The present book follows a similar path moving from metaphor to symbol, and finding a way into the depth of symbol through artistic imagery. Paul Ricoeur recognizes a stable, metaphoric process, or a root metaphor:

> Metaphorical functioning would be completely inadequate as a way of expressing the different temporality of symbols, what we might call their insistence, if metaphors did not save themselves

> from complete evanescence by means of a whole array of intersignifications. One metaphor, in effect, calls for another and each one stays alive by conserving its power to evoke the whole network. The network engenders what we can call root metaphors. [Ricoeur, 1976: 64].

One aspect of a metaphoric network approximates even more closely what we mean here by root metaphor. In the quotation above, Ricoeur identifies metaphoric clusters which persist in a particular tradition; for example, different ways in which the divine mystery is metaphorically interpreted in a religious tradition: Jesus as king, shepherd, savior, servant, etc. He also notes that sets of metaphors, as Philip Wheelwright has argued, develop on various levels of organization, "depending on whether we consider the metaphors in isolated sentences, or as underlying a given poem, or as the dominant metaphors of a poet, or the typical metaphors of a particular linguistic community or a given culture, which can extend so far as to include large cultural spheres such as Christianity" (Ricoeur, 1976: 65).

Now, all of this preoccupation with metaphor is itself an indicator of a cultural shift in root metaphors in our time. Artistic process is not reducible to metaphor, of course, but metaphor is of the very essence of that process. John Dixon has drawn attention to this phenomenon in his book *Art and the Theological Imagination*. Metaphor, he observes, is the "linking of apparently different things by some profoundly felt connection between them" (Dixon: 12). He identifies the unity of metaphor and art: "Thus, the making of the work of art is basically a metaphoric activity, the penetration into the secret life of things to find the bonds between them" (Dixon: 12). Further, contrary to the thinking of a mechanistic age, "Art is not an ornament to an existing world, it is the primary means of *forming the world*" (Dixon: 12; italics added).

This is why I have chosen artistic process as the most appropriate root metaphor for a creative age such as our own. Whatever the limitations of the technological era, it knows itself as a transformative power in nature and history. But art is also the bonding of humanity and nature, a bonding which has eroded in the mechanistic age. For both of these reasons artistic process as metaphor and the metaphoric power that informs artistic process furnish important clues to understanding both the *powers* and *limits* of the modern age.

ARTISTIC PROCESS

Interpretations of artistic process have varied over the course of Western history, even as the arts have been understood very differently among different cultures and peoples. Classical Greece gave a significant place to all of the arts; nevertheless, classical philosophy ranked artistic creation very low on the scale of wisdom and truth. In that perspective the arts produced copies of things, even lower in the hierarchy of being than the earthly things which were copies of the eternal forms. Hence, the arts produced that which was lowest in the order of being and knowledge. Since arts such as poetics and music could touch the senses in ways that might corrupt, a metaphysician like Plato held the arts in disdain and even distrust. At the same time, the arts created things of beauty which could elevate the soul to higher things, opening a pathway to a vision of truth.[6] This ambivalence toward the arts can be traced through the course of organicist thinking in the classical and Christian eras. The arts were useful, and even at times ennobling, but they mediated neither knowledge nor wisdom; hence, arts were ranked with crafts.

Only toward the middle of the Renaissance do we find the artist recognized as distinct from other craftspeople (Blunt: 48ff.). Subsequently the transformation in appreciation of artistic process receives further impetus from the emerging mechanistic understanding of nature. In the early period of Enlightenment, during the seventeenth and eighteenth centuries, the arts were understood as presentations of the order of things, following rules of natural order and reproducing that order in esthetic form (Cassirer: chap. 7). In the late eighteenth and nineteenth centuries, nature was conceived as a rational order, knowable only in the categories of the subject, unknowable in itself. The arts furnished a clue to the sublime moral purpose of that rational order, but only in terms of subjective appreciation.[7] Thus the art of genius and the genius of esthetic sensibility emerge gradually, removing art from everyday life and displacing it into museums and concert halls for the appreciation of the elite of the bourgeois age. An esthetics of subjective appreciation and objectified art of a high culture originally produced a counterpoint to spreading industrialism, science, and technical process. But gradually artistic process in this mechanical age was displaced to the periphery, and esthetic values were ensconced in the salons of the bourgeoisie.

A new transformation in the interpretation of the arts occurred in the twentieth century. The arts challenged the hegemony of the technological order, first in the work of the romantic poets, later in the invasion of forms and order in painting, sculpture, poetics, and music (Roszak: pt. 3). Most critics mark this breakthrough in painting with the work of Cezanne (Dixon: 128ff.). The twentieth century opened with a burst of metaphoric creativity in all fields, challenging the mind of a mechanistic age even in the realm of physics which had been its fortress. Creative scientists were leaving mechanism behind even as it gained plausibility in the human sciences and public mind. Artists led the way in breaking this new ground, although interestingly it was through cubism that they opened entirely new paths. Paul Klee is a striking exemplar of this process, and I shall return to his creative contributions to this new artistic vision. For the moment, it may suffice to say that he was able to synthesize mechanistic and organicist images in a vision of creation into a higher order, thus providing a path toward a new, more human world. The modern world will not eschew technology, except as the result of a nuclear debacle. And a totally organicist world is alien to the modern age except in the case of a primitivistic totalitarianism of the kind that captivated Nazi Germany. This leaves one principal option for the contemporary Westernized world: to accept gratefully its creative powers; to comprehend how these powers may be modes of attunement to nature and knowledge rather than modes of domination and exploitation. It is my thesis that artistic process best provides just such an integration of organic and mechanistic processes in creative dwelling. But before taking up in detail the nature of that integrative process, it is necessary to look further at the metaphoric power of creative disclosure that the arts and artistic process both generate and symbolize. Indeed, the entire method of this book—as has already been adumbrated in all of the preceding discussion—is a dialectic of socio-historical understanding and of artistic activity, particularly as the latter has been discerned by its major theoreticians and practitioners. It is my assumption—rather my conviction—that it is by this interplay, this to-fro movement (itself metaphoric in the largest sense) that the nature of the present crisis of modern technological society may be discerned and, I would hope, somewhat resolved.

Among the philosophic interpreters of the place of the arts, none have been more insightful than John Dewey and Hans-Georg Gadamer. I shall return to John Dewey's work, whose explication of method in artistic process seems unrivaled in our time. Hans-Georg Gadamer, on the other hand, unfolds an understanding of the work of art in a way that articulates with the present writer's concern for symbols and history. Although he does not emphasize metaphor, Gadamer interprets artistic process as an analogy through which we can understand history and language.

Hans-Georg Gadamer states his interpretation of the work of art very simply:

> The specific mode of the work of art's presence is the coming into representation of being. [Gadamer: 142]

This proposition can only be understood within the total context of Gadamer's vision. Gadamer's point of departure is the notion of play, itself being dialectical, an expression of the to-fro movement of life and nature. Following Johan Huizinga's thought in his seminal *Homo Ludens,* Gadamer sees play as the way of being of bios and cosmos. Huizinga himself had traced the origins of culture and civilization to play (Huizinga: 46–63). For Gadamer play becomes culture as an artistic achievement. In this sense, art is rooted in the character of life itself as play. Play is the way of being of things, and art is the re-presentation of this being in intelligible forms. Gadamer notes that life presents itself in its play; in this sense, art is a carrying forth of this presentation in a re-presentation that makes bios and cosmos accessible to a world of meaning.

> The fact that the mode of being of play is so close to the mobile form of nature permits us to make an important methodological conclusion. It is obviously not correct to say that animals too play and that we can even say metaphorically that water and light play. Rather, on the contrary, we can say that man too plays. His playing is a natural process. The meaning of his play, precisely because—and insofar as—he is part of nature, is a pure self-presentation. Thus it becomes finally meaningless to distinguish in this sphere between literal and metaphorical usage. [Gadamer: 94]

I shall later argue that art and play, as metaphorical interpretations of the cosmos and the human species, illumine the being of things and human creativity. This seems to be the implication of Gadamer's use of the term *literal* in the above quotation.

In developing his case for artistic process as the most apt metaphor for human species life, Gadamer distinguishes play from art. Here he follows Johan Huizinga who is very explicit on this point. Huizinga, conceiving of art as closest to the way of being of play, rejects any simple identification. He puts it thus:

> Many and close are the links that connect play with beauty. All the same, we cannot say that beauty is inherent in play as such; so we must leave it at that: Play is a function of the living, but is not susceptible of exact definition either logically, biologically, or aesthetically. The play-concept must always remain distinct from all the other forms of thought in which we express the structure of mental and social life. [Huizinga: 7]

Huizinga's reservation about definitions of play points to the primordiality of this notion, bringing it close to the notion of Being in Western thought, connecting with Plato's identification of play with holiness.[8]

Hans-Georg Gadamer follows Huizinga rather closely in moving from primordial play to the game, and then to dramatic or artistic process. Huizinga identifies two aspects of play which lead to higher forms in ritual and the arts:

> The function of play in the higher forms which concern us here can largely be derived from the two basic aspects under which we meet it: as a contest *for* something or a representation *of* something. These two functions can unite in such a way that the game "represents" a contest, or else becomes a contest for the best representation of something. [Huizinga: 13]

Along a similar line, Gadamer begins with the contest or game, then proceeds to re-presentation in dramatic action. Thus, he establishes the links between primordial play, the play of the game, dramatic action as a play, and other modes of artistic representation.

Several elements of the game furnish links between play and drama. In a game like baseball, it is evident that the game includes players and spectators. In Gadamer's words, the real subject of the game is not the players or spectators, but the game itself. This seems a trivial point, but it defines the world which players and spectators enter when the game is played. Players who distract attention from the contest by grandstanding detract from the game. Spectators who run onto the field and hold up the game spoil the play. In brief, the game masters players and spectators when it is properly played. The game tests and tries the players, rather than the reverse.

Further, games define a space, a pattern of motion and relations among the players through rules which govern the game. The area of the game, its boundaries, the appropriate directions of movement, are structured by the rules of the game. The game guides players and spectators through its structure, yet that structure is only structure in being played, in the dynamic unfolding of play. The structure is play, even as play is structure. This dynamic understanding of the reciprocity of play and structure is a fundamental notion in Gadamer's interpretation of the work of art. It is for this reason that I have spoken of the work of art and the artistic process as interchangeable, for the work is a dynamic event, a playing out of structure.

Art is distinct from play in that it is representation for someone else. A drama, for example, is a re-presentation of the play of life for an audience. The religious rite reenacts a sacred myth or event for the participants. Playing on behalf of an audience is characteristic of art and distinguishes it from the self-presentation of nature and the play of the game. The drama provides a helpful transition from game to art in this movement from the play of nature through the game to artistic process. The way of being of the players undergoes a marked change in the dramatic form. In the drama, as Gadamer notes, the spectators become the players. The spectators reproduce the drama which the actors are representing. This view of the audience contrasts with the usual way of interpreting dramatic action. There is a tendency in some perspectives to treat the drama as it is played by the actors as a thing in itself. Gadamer identifies the audience as the fourth wall of the dramatic space, pointing out that the dynamic structure of the unfolding play becomes event in its reproduction through the participation of the audience. This importance of the audience has been noted recently in the American theatre where much has been made of its role.

Thus, Hans-Georg Gadamer establishes the continuity and discontinuity of play, the game, and artistic process. His aim is to lift up the role of the audience in all artistic process, thus preserving the reproductive character of the artistic event whether in drama, musical composition, poem, or architectural work. For Gadamer, art is always performance. The work of art is not an object in isolation. The work of art is a dynamic structure which has its being in being played, in its reproduction. Gadamer is trying to break away from the "esthetic" perspective which treats the work of art as an esthetic object over against the subject, as an object to be viewed and appreciated in abstraction from the transforming dynamics of reproduction.

This understanding of the work of art as a dynamic event applies across the board for Gadamer, although it is somewhat more obvious in the drama. The musical composition has its being in being played and heard. The poetic text lives in the performative understanding of hearers or readers. The work of art is, then, artistic event or process which *is* in re-presentation and re-production. This is not to suggest that the work of art lacks wholeness or structure, for the work is transformation of play into structure.

> Play is structure—this means that despite its dependence on being played it is a meaningful whole which can be repeatedly represented as such and the significance of which can be understood. But the structure is also play, because—despite this theoretical unity—it achieves its full being only each time it is played. It is the complementary nature of the two sides of the one thing that we seek to underline, as against the abstraction of aesthetic differentiation. [Gadamer: 105]

This understanding of the work of art is more appropriately expressed in English as *artistic event* or *artistic process,* and so I have used these terms wherever possible.

We have already identified the structural character of the artistic event in Gadamer's thought but something more needs to be said about this aspect. Art is the transformation of play into structure (*die Gebilde*). The drama, for example, has plot, characterizations, and dénouement which are intended, repeatable, and intelligible. This dynamic process of the work has an ideality which Gadamer calls structure. By transformation Gadamer means more than a change in which something persists yet alters in quality. Transformation means that "something is suddenly and as a whole something else, that this other transformed thing that it has become is its true being, in comparison with which its earlier being is nothing" (Gadamer: 100). The same event or figure can lend itself to many artistic expressions and modes. The work of art transforms these possibilities into a meaningful whole which, when successful, is revelatory of the true being of the event or figure. The measure of truth in the work is in its disclosing, revelatory power—a power which is tested again and again as the work is reenacted by the viewer, reader, or audience.

Knowledge is an essential ingredient of artistic process in this perspective. The reenactment of the work includes feelings, moods, sensation, and a variety of other modes of experience, but knowledge is a crucial aspect. Artistic process is, in this sense, a total experiencing of the world disclosed in the work. This is the fuller implication of the notion of "transformation into structure.'' The re-presentation of what *is* in its true being is the essence of the artistic event. Hence, Gadamer's statement with which we opened this exposition of his view of the work of art: ''The specific mode of the work of art's presence is the coming into representation of being'' (Gadamer: 142).

The socio-historical character of the artistic event has been assumed in all that has been said thus far. A drama is a revelatory event, disclosing the play of human life in an understandable structure, yet persisting over time and subject to ever new re-presentations and re-productions. The drama is always new in these re-presentations, yet it preserves a continuity as a structure for those interpretations. Hence, there is continuity of structure and discontinuity of interpretation in the dyanamic, historical event of the work of art. A similar continuity and discontinuity occur in the audience by whom the artistic event is reenacted. The work draws the audience out of itself into an ecstatic self-forgetfulness, yet in the successful work the audience is at the same time reconciled to itself on a deeper level of experience. This is most evident in the religious rite but applies to any artistic event in differing degrees.

Hans-Georg Gadamer slights the role of artists in his interpretation of artistic process because he is reacting against subjective esthetics and the psychologizing of historical interpretation in the work of Dilthey and his followers. He is also reacting against the cult of genius which stressed the subjective, noncognitive character of art. However, artistic process includes the artist as well as the audience, although the artist releases the work to the public. This invests the work with freedom from the author. Cole Porter is said to have experienced this letting go whenever one of his musicals opened; after the opening he thought of the work as something outside of himself. Artistic events do, in fact, presuppose esthetic sensitivity in the creators and the participants, yet works possess an autonomy beyond the intentions of authors and original audiences. This is the important point which Gadamer stresses in unfolding the historicality of the work of art. Its structure furnishes a criterion of correct interpretation, yet its representation is always part of a new epoch. The interpretative task is evaded by attempting to recreate the original in abstraction from contemporary meanings and understandings, as though playing *Hamlet* in original dress would somehow capture the meaning of the work as originally intended. The work of art comes to presence through re-presentation in contemporary life and thought, even as its original appearance belonged to an historical context. In this respect, the artistic event is ever new and enriched in each reproduction.

Gadamer's interpretation of the work of art employs drama as its first example. However, there are important differences in the arts which Gadamer has explored. The richness of artistic process as root metaphor rests in part on the variety of modes of artistic disclosure. Gadamer lays the stress finally on language and the text, or literature, as the artistic work par excellence. This emphasis on literature derives primarily from his concern with history and hermeneutics. Yet other arts illumine various aspects of human dwelling, disclosing the revelatory power of the arts in distinctive ways. Architecture plays a crucial role in enspacing human dwelling, giving it boundaries and meaningful orientations in the world. Sculpture discloses the deeper powers and movements of space and line. Painting discloses deep structures of the world by line, color, and texture, illumining nature and life. Musical composition gives form to the rhythms and movements of life process, bringing past and future to presence in a total experience. These and other art forms are independent sources of illumination and deepening of life. In this view of human dwelling as artistic process, I have been insisting that the arts proper play a significant role as creative clues to human possibilities. The special contribution of the arts proper is to keep open the world of human dwelling amidst inertial forces of routinization. Although we shall focus on artistic process as metaphoric image, the importance of the arts proper as modes of disclosure is always in the background. Artistic process is paradigmatic for human dwelling because it forms and renews the world.

Although Hans-Georg Gadamer treats literature as the artistic event par excellence, he draws on painting in order to interpret truth in the work of art. His most telling example of this power of artistic disclosure is portraiture. The representation of the royal figure exemplifies the being of the work of art. A portrait is something quite different from a copy of the figure of the subject. It creates the imperial figure which the original then takes as a clue to its own stance and being. As Gadamer observes,

> The picture then has an independence that also affects the original. For strictly speaking it is only through the picture that the original becomes the original picture, i.e. it is the picture that makes what is represented into a picture. . . . It is because the ruler, the statesman and the hero must show and present himself to his followers, because he must represent, that the picture gains its own reality. Nevertheless, there is here a turning-point. When he shows himself he must fulfil the expectation that his picture arouses. Only because he has part of his being in showing himself is he represented in the picture. First, then, there is undoubtedly self-representation, and secondly the representation in the picture of this self-representation. Pictorial representation is a special case of public representation. But the second has an effect on the first. . . . Paradoxical as it may sound, the original becomes a picture only through the picture, and yet the picture is nothing but the appearance of the original. [Gadamer: 125f.]

Gadamer discerns the disclosure of being in the work of art as the truth of the work. This is the accomplishment of artistic representation. So Gadamer will say,

> The world which appears in the play of representation does not stand like a copy next to the real world, but it is the latter in the heightened truth of its being. [Gadamer: 121]

Thus we return to John Dixon's assertion that art is the power to mediate the fullness of nature and life in humanly revelatory forms. Creation and re-creation become one in the artistic process where the play of life and cosmos come to re-presentation in the heightened truth of their being.

ARTISTIC PROCESS AS ROOT METAPHOR

Gadamer's interpretation of the work of art sets the stage for his hermeneutical approach to history. He takes the literary text as the work of art par excellence. His choice of literature and the text rests upon the communicability of the text, though this preference in no way depreciates the richness of the world of various forms of art. The text, moreover, forms the principal source or subject matter for historical interpretation, so the text is the appropriate form of art for his project. Since he has established that representation of the work of art involves reproductive participation by the audience, he can use this model for understanding the hermeneutical task of interpreting a tradition. The interpreter of the tradition understands the historical text by reproductive participation, involving the contemporary world of the interpreter as well as the meaning projected in the text. Much more needs to be said about this question of historical interpretation, and I shall return to it in chapter 3. The question for the moment is the sense in which artistic process can function as a root metaphor. Does Gadamer's interpretation of the work of art provide a model or paradigm of artistic process as root metaphor? There is no question that Gadamer intends reproduction of the work of art to function as an analogy to interpreting an historical tradition. In what sense is he drawing on a metaphoric understanding of artistic process?

Analogy and metaphor have the common element of drawing upon similarities for understanding the less known from the better known. However, tensive metaphors are much more than this, since they conjoin similar and dissimilar realities in an explosive disclosure of insight. This is the paradoxical quality of the tensive metaphor. A metaphor thus resolves a contradiction in an unexpected way which generates new understanding. The basic question, then, is whether one is moving on a deeper level than analogy when one construes a hermeneutics of history from the structure of artistic work and its reproduction.

Analogy is an abstract way of talking about a working metaphor, since analogy draws upon a conjunction in things which is discerned in reflection. However, analogy draws out the similarity in the metaphoric imagery, letting the dissimilarity fall into the background. In this sense, analogy functions as a weakened metaphor. By contrast, Gadamer views the work of art as a dynamic event. The work of art functions in his proposal as what

I have called a root metaphor. It furnishes a guide to the coherence of the world or the meaning of history.

It is, as I have noted, paradoxical to turn to artistic process for a paradigm for the historicality of human dwelling when a mechanistic metaphor holds such a dominant position in the modern world. It is, after all, the productive application of science and technical discovery which has made the modern world a powerful, if at times destructive, agency in history. But it is precisely this paradox which discloses the appropriateness of artistic process for interpreting human history in this modern age. The difference between artistic and techno-scientific process is obvious and striking. The arts work with images that convey multiple and sometimes paradoxical meanings, generating moods and insights, opening horizons that had not been glimpsed. By contrast, the techno-scientific process seeks for precision of concepts, determination of conditions and outcomes, and stipulation of univocal meanings. The arts generate insight through imagery and ambiguity. The techno-scientific orientation seeks understanding through analytic procedures that can establish manageable areas of inquiry, leading to prediction and control. The common element between artistic process and techno-scientific work is, of course, language; however, the two modes of thinking and working develop different modes of discourse. Philip Wheelwright draws a useful distinction here between the steno-discourse of scientific inquiry and the expressive discourse of poetic process. In Wheelwright's interpretation, both modes of discourse have referential significance, disclosing realities and yielding understanding. However, techno-scientific discourse yields univocal, conventional, and stipulated meanings, while poetic or expressive discourse yields ambiguous, deep, paradoxical, and plural realms of meaning.

If the differences between artistic process and techno-scientific discourse are so striking, it seems *utterly* paradoxical to turn to artistic process to guide thought and action in the modern, technologized world. However, there is a deeper common element which makes artistic process a powerful metaphoric guide for the modern age. Artistic process and techno-scientific discourse are bound together on the deepest level through metaphoric power. This is the inner bond of similarity which is concealed in many scientific endeavors. Further, the striking phenomenon of the modern age is the disclosure of the human capacity to enter creatively into the formation of nature as well as history. The human now knows itself to be a creative, if also limited and finite, agency in life and cosmos. If this were not already evident in the latter half of the twentieth century, space travel and the splitting of DNA would have made the case beyond any question. It is this creative element that is the source of power in different realms of discourse. Metaphor is the common element in these various fields of thought and action. In Robert Nisbet's telling words,

> It is easy to dismiss metaphor as "unscientific" or "non-rational," a mere substitute for the hard analysis that rigorous thought requires . . . but metaphor belongs to philosophy and even to science. It is clear from many studies of the cognitive process generally, and particularly of creative thought that the act of thought in its more intense phases is often inseparable from metaphor—from that intuitive, iconic, encapsulating grasp of a new entity or process. [Nisbet: 5]

The root metaphor of artistic process thus conjoins the different regions of human life and thought in a common, creative power of metaphoric disclosure. One begins to sense the artistic, creative character of the human species in building its dwelling and letting a world of meanings and possibilities come to light. The techno-scientific process readily obscures this artistic quality, especially since much of its creative effort is harnessed to industrial and military organizations. Nevertheless, the deeper reality of human dwelling is that it thrives upon creative, metaphoric disclosures and decays when such powers degenerate into mechanical repetition.

The contrast between mechanical repetition and metaphoric creativity is a clue to the promise of artistic process for a technological world. The forces of productive expansion are exhausting the resources of our fragile earth, yet the world seems on the march to ever increasing productivity. The destructive forces of nuclear violence threaten the annihilation of all life on the earth, yet the national security states seem locked in an upward spiral of competition for superiority in arms. This is a degeneration of a civilization that contrasts with the slow decay of some earlier peoples. However, it is the decay that sets in with mechanical repetition, doing over and over again the very things that are proving most destructive to the well-being of peoples. Artistic process and the metaphoric power it discloses are the modes of freedom and transcendence which release peoples from such mechanical repetition. Artistic creativity opens worlds that have not been glimpsed or experienced. Practical creativity in politics and economics opens new possibilities of dwelling, refusing to settle for decay and repetition. Metaphoric insights in science, philosophy, religion, and morality open vistas of humanization which had not been imagined. Here, transcendence means an inner, historical distancing from the determining forces that encompass human dwelling. Art is the creative distancing of an inner-historical transcendence. Artistic process is a power of transcending and liberation for which this age yearns in its agony of self-destruction.

Walker Percy identifies this artistic power of liberation in the opening paragraph of "The Man on the Train":

> There is no such thing, strictly speaking, as a literature of alienation. In the re-presenting of alienation the category is reversed and becomes something entirely different. There is a great deal of difference between an alienated commuter riding a train and this same commuter reading a book about an alienated commuter riding a train. . . . The nonreading commuter exists in true alienation, which is unspeakable; the reading commuter rejoices in the speakability of his alienation and in the new triple alliance of himself, the alienated character, and the author. His mood is affirmatory and glad: Yes! that is how it is!—which is an aesthetic reversal of alienation. It is related that when Kafka read his work aloud to his friends they would all roar with laughter until tears came to their eyes. Neither Kafka nor his reader is alienated in the movement of art, for each achieves a reversal through its re-presenting. To picture a truly alienated man, picture a Kafka to whom it has never occurred to write a word. [Percy: 83]

The root metaphor of artistic process, then, holds some promise of transcending the incoherence and anarchy of the mechanistic age. Metaphors do not settle everything, but they are guides to the rich possibilities of life and nature. When the decay of mechanical determinations holds a people in bondage, as seems to be the case in the technological order, we depend upon such metaphoric power to open a horizon of possibilities, with a vision to judge and liberate our age.

This deeper level of liberated human capacity, the metaphoric power of creative disclosure, leads back again to the theme of play with which Gadamer's inquiry begins. The play of life and cosmos, the self-presentation of life in its play, is the ultimate source of the arts, sciences, and other modes of human activity. Johan Huizinga formulated this insight, noting:

> The great archetypal activities of human society are all permeated with play from the start. Take language, for instance—that first and supreme instrument which man shapes in order to communicate, to teach, to command. Language allows him to distinguish, to establish, to state things; in short, to name them and by naming them to raise them into the domain of the spirit. In the making of speech and language the spirit is continually "sparking" between matter and mind, as it were, playing with this wondrous nominative faculty. Behind every abstract expression there lie the boldest of metaphors, and every metaphor is a play upon words. Thus in giving expression to life man creates a second, poetic world alongside the world of nature. [Huizinga: 4]

Huizinga's brilliant insight into the play of nature and the play of language undergirds Gadamer's project, though it is never formulated in quite this way. To be sure, Gadamer has a somewhat deeper understanding of the role of language, although he concurs in Huizinga's interpretation of the role of metaphor in the creative work of language (Gadamer: 389). This is precisely his understanding of the transformation into structure of the artistic event. Hence, metaphor and metaphoric power constitute the correspondence that generates the tensive metaphor of artistic process.

These reflections on artistic process developed around several themes. The conflict between traditional societies and the technologized world was interpreted through the medium of opposing root metaphors, organicism and mechanism. It was claimed that these metaphors provided clues to the total world views that meet in these contending societies. The mechanistic age has proved to be so destructive of nature and life that there seemed to be little reason to dismiss the claims of traditional peoples as irrelevant. The conflict of these worlds was also found within the mechanistic societies, for they seem to live with both metaphors. The technological societies operate with mechano-morphic images in politico-economic organization yet preserve organicist hierarchies of male dominance in familial, religious, and interpersonal communities. Hence, the sexist oppression of industrial societies reflects the dialectic of mechanism and organicism that is threatening traditional peoples throughout the world.

The artistic metaphor offers some important insights through which these conflicts may be transcended. Art is no respecter of persons, though male dominance in the West forced a suppression of women's contributions in art for many centuries. The image of the human being as artist belongs to men and women as human beings in the image of God. There is nothing essentially sexist about the artistry of the human species. In a particular era or cultural epoch, men and women may express their artistry in different modes and activities, but the virtue of these creative activities implies no difference in authority and worth. In the technologized age, differences of biological strength or force become less and less relevant, similarities in creative power and capacity become ever more important. However, the transformation of human dwelling requires more than metaphoric clues. It demands different institutional arrangements, new patterns of relationship, innovative modes of education. Traditional peoples are struggling for a new world that is more than the sterile, inhuman exchanges of a mechanistic age. Women are striving for an equality that is more than grudging acceptance into the arid corridors of bureaucratic efficiency. These contending forces point toward a new society, even as the self-destructive tendencies of the mechanistic age demand a new, more humane order of existence.

Metaphors furnish clues to transformation, but they are not the powers that resist or engender such new realities. A people's history or dwelling is founded in symbol and language. This is the peculiar character of the human species. It is a symbolizing species. Instincts and biological impulses continue to play an important role in human activities but only on an elemental level. Human activity is shaped by cultural models and linguistic modes of activity. It is as though the human species, as it emerged on the evolutionary stage, came into being with and through language and tools, creating its own kinds of instincts through its linguistic activities and patterns of relationship. The unifying powers of this human event, historical dwelling, are the symbols that gather the activities into shared communities. Symbols of family and kin, work and play, neighborhood and governance, moral order and religious world—these are the shared meanings that hold a people together over time, preserving its identity and sustaining its hope in the future. Symbols are the powers that resist change or open the way to creative change when it is needed. Root metaphors are interpretations of these founding symbols.

This is a second step in unfolding the role of artistic metaphor in illumining human dwelling. In contrast to mechanism, artistic process raises the symbol to its true significance in human life. The suppression of symbol by the mechanistic age was delineated in the introduction to this volume. It was suggested that this suppression is actually a concealment of the distorted symbolization that holds sway in the mechanistic world. By the same token, artistic process discloses the centrality of symbol in the artistry of dwelling. To this extent, ascendancy of artistic process is a sign of the rediscovery of symbols in our time.

Dwelling comes to coherence and continuity in the symbolizations which found it and shape its possibilities. This is the crucial event of disclosure and historical formation around which human dwelling gathers. It is a linguistic event in the sense that all things human come to be in meanings that can be articulated in discourse. However, symbols are richer and more complex than other modes of discourse. They are linguistic events which conjoin several levels of experience as I shall try to make clear in chapter 2. The term *language* does not convey adequately what is analogous to artistic process in historical dwelling. Language founds dwelling in symbols. However, symbols unfold day by day in various activities and patterned modes of action. Symbols are lived through an interpretative process of thinking, feeling, doing, making, and deciding. These lived interpretations are crystallized in various modes which we shall explicate in chapter 3.

I noted above that three comprehensive metaphors of the properly human have competed for dominance in Western life, and I am proposing that the unfolding of human powers in our own time makes artistic process a more fitting image of the ways of human dwelling. I am also arguing that the destructive potential of organicist and mechanistic imagery creates a situation in which new metaphoric insight is desperately needed. This is not to say that organicism and mechanism are simply displaced by a new root metaphor. Artistic process incorporates organicist and mechanistic elements in a world more human than anything human history has yet revealed. The interplay of parts in organic wholes is crucial to any work of art. In the realm of dwelling, mechanistic processes play a significant role, even as organic, life processes are integral to all human relationships. The aim here is not to displace all other imagery but to relocate these other images in more appropriate places within the authentic process of human dwelling. Thus, the creativity and self-transcending power of human species life in history and language can be liberated from the oppressive forces of mechanism and the nostalgic yearning for traditional, organic bonds of blood and soil. We are attending to the creative powers of human species life and, so far as we speak of history, we are seeing the human venture as cocreation with the source of life. This sets a context of responsibility for human species life both within the cosmic realm of creation and in the historical realm of justice and peace.

Artistic process is a metaphoric understanding which places priority on creativity. But history also involves continuity, memory, and tradition. Thus, we may seem to be undermining the continuities of human dwelling by placing so much emphasis on the creative powers of self-transcendence and the dynamic, changing character of experience. This is only an apparent problem, however, for historical continuities are constituted by the symbols which gather and preserve human life over time.

NOTES

1. The organicist imagery of life and cosmos is delineated in its principal lines and variety by John A. Wilson and Thorkild Jacobsen in *The Intellectual Adventure of Ancient Man* (Frankfort et al.: chaps. 2–7). Different versions of this organicist imagery are drawn together into universal patterns by Mircea Eliade in his various works and especially in *Patterns in Comparative Religion* (Eliade, 1958). The author is indebted to Stuart McLean for his work on root metaphors.

2. A variety of materials on the environmental crisis were gathered in *The Environmental Handbook* (DeBell). Essays on the cultural and moral aspects of the crisis are to be found in *Ecology and Religion in History* (Spring and Spring).

3. The struggle to cope with these corrosive forces is documented in *People, Building Neighborhoods* (The National Commission on Neighborhoods).

4. The mechanistic imagery is already dominant in the thought of René Descartes who envisioned the body as a machine and of Thomas Hobbes for whom reality is composed of entitative forces; see also the discussion by Elizabeth Sewell (Sewell: 68ff.).

5. Archetypal energies are used to refer to directionalities in bios and cosmos which come to structure in human dwelling. Mircea Eliade has identified many of these archetypal directionalities in his study of universal patterns in religion (Eliade, 1958: 32f.; Eliade, 1959). Philip Wheelwright has also explored these perduring patterns (Wheelwright, 1962: chap. 6; 1968: chap. 7).

6. Martin Heidegger explored the ambiguity of Plato's interpretation of the relation of art to truth, disclosing the problematic of truth which this ambiguity concealed (Heidegger, 1979: 163–99).

7. Hans-Georg Gadamer devotes pt. 1 of his work to tracing this movement to the subjectivisation of art in the differentiation of the esthetic object (Gadamer: 39–73).

8. Johan Huizinga traces the primordiality of play and its place in veneration of the deity. Play in this primordial sense is a prominent theme in the later work of Heidegger (Heidegger, 1971: 179–82).

2

METAPHOR AND SYMBOL

FOR several generations, social scientists and historians of religion have recognized the importance of symbols. However, the foundational role of symbols is somewhat obscured by the mechanistic paradigm which has dominated these fields of inquiry in the twentieth century. With notable exceptions such as Mircea Eliade, symbolization of bios and cosmos has been viewed as either an archaic stage of human experience or a deviation from rational, practical thinking as a consequence of personal or social strain (Baum). These deconstructions of symbol have been useful in liberating thought from the dogmatic power of distorted symbolizations; at the same time, they have obscured the centrality and continuing vitality of symbolization in human history. The artistic paradigm supports this critical approach to symbols as I shall attempt to demonstrate in chapter 3. However, the artistic metaphor also discloses the foundational place of symbols in human dwelling. Symbols are, in fact, metaphoric events that arise through the poetic powers of the human species. However, these metaphoric works reveal the archetypal movements of bios and cosmos. Symbols speak, as Ricoeur observes, because the cosmos speaks. In this respect, human dwelling is founded by symbolic disclosures in artistic process.

Anselm Strauss once posed the question of what it means to say that one is a member of a group or community. After considering such possibilities as going to meetings, being on a list of members, being recognized as a member, he proposed that membership is essentially a question of shared symbolism (Strauss). Members of a group participate in a common symbolic world that weaves together the multiplicity of threads which bind them to one another. In this context, he reflected on the problems of ethnic identity and the power which symbols exercise in groups.

Toward the end of his career, Alfred Schutz also investigated group identities and symbolism. This material was presented in an important essay, "Symbol, Reality and Society" (Schutz, 1962: 287–356). His theory of society started with the consciousness of the actor in the world—what Paul Tillich called the "self and world correlation." But this perspective involves serious difficulties for sociology, since it fails to account for memberships which transcend the individual consciousness, memberships such as families and communities. If each person belongs to social groupings only on the basis of some conscious orientation, then all such societal groupings appear to be mere aggregates of different interests and perspectives. For example, my sister and I may view our family as *our* family, but she lives in her consciousness, experiencing one family to which she belongs, while I live in my consciousness, experiencing quite a different family. We may talk with each other at some length about the family and end up with agreements about *our* family, but this is a consensus which we fabricate. The same would hold for religious communities, neighborhoods, or other groupings that extend beyond a person's particular consciousness. Thus, Alfred Schutz was wrestling with the question of the other person's consciousness, a questionable reality if the only starting-point is one's own consciousness, and, by the same token, equally questionable for the reality of any grouping beyond one's own consciousness (Schutz, 1962: 150–203).

Schutz thought for a time that he had resolved the question of membership in groups through his notion of the "We-relation"—or intimate, face-to-face relationship. His theory of the "We" was built around personal encounters in which the Self and the Other—much as in Martin Buber's "I and Thou" relation—experience each other's presence as an immediate datum. He spoke of this as a "tuning in" relationship of simultaneous, inner time consciousness. This was an intuitional notion of encounter which he drew from Henri Bergson's theory of *durée* or inner temporality (Schutz, 1962: 172–79). Members of a We-relation, thus, share a simultaneity of inner time consciousness. Yet such immediate presence can only be an evanescent event. Most of the time one is conscious of the other person as friend or husband or wife, objectified in what Schutz called typifications or roles. Such ideal typifications were obviously constructions. This means that the We-relation is a transitory encounter in a world of typifications. Alfred Schutz's theory of marriage, family, ethnic community, neighborhood, church, nation, or any grouping beyond the evanescent We-relation would then be a typifying construction with only a semblance of reality.

Schutz's problem in accounting for communal groupings gave rise to two opposing approaches in sociology. Harold Garfinkel and his colleagues, in what is called ethnomethodology, developed the radically individualistic aspect of Schutz's theory (Garfinkel: 1–34). Thomas Luckmann and Peter Berger took Schutz's theory in the opposite direction, arguing that society is a construction of typifications which are later imposed upon new members through socialization, enclosing people in a social world over against their particular consciousnesses (Berger and Luckmann: chaps. 1–4). Like ethnomethodology, Berger and Luckmann accept individual consciousness as a starting-point, but they resolve the problem of communal groupings by treating it as an imposed consensus. Social reality was fashioned by treating society as an alien imposition: a massive "I and It" structure against which the spontaneous ego is powerless.

Schutz's failure to resolve the solipsistic question of the isolated consciousness provided support for each of these two, subsequently developed perspectives. However, his work on symbolism, only partially unfolded before his death, opened a way beyond the radical individualism which he appropriated from Max Weber's sociology and Edmund Husserl's philosophy. Individualism and collectivism have been the Scylla and Charybdis of sociology from the outset (Winter, 1963). Schutz finally transcended this dichotomy in his theory of symbols.

After identifying various modes of signifying in human communication—marks, indications, signs—Schutz argued that symbols mediate such higher order experiences as group memberships or scientific inquiries, experiences reaching beyond everyday, empirical realities. He argued that symbols cluster around everyday things which are associated with higher order meanings. Thus, hearth and home are everyday, situational materials associated with family life; for example, the word *family* is etymologically rooted in the notion of dwelling-place. Further, *home* in the English language often serves for the complex reality of one's family. These familial symbolizations gradually play into higher order realities such as homeland, mother country, and fatherland. In a similar way, Native Americans have often identified their tribal reality with the land in which they dwelt for hunting, gathering, or cultivating. Perceptible things in our everyday world, thus, become vehicles for higher order symbolizations which then found memberships and identities. The issue that Schutz explores is how such everyday things can mediate higher order meanings which preserve a people's identity over the course of history (Mol: chap. 5).

Alfred Schutz employs the mechanism of appresentation to explain how everyday things become symbols of higher order meanings. Edmund Husserl used the mechanism of appresentation to account for perception. He rejected the notion that perception was simply a reception of sense data internally organized in an apperceptual process of consciousness, and argued that perception is a meaning-conferring act which intends a totality, as when one perceives a lamp, one only senses the surface of the lamp, yet perceives a whole lamp. The process by which one fills up the sense impressions with the total object, its other side, its full shape, etc., is an analogizing act of imagination. This analogizing act appresents the unsensed portions which are not directly present. The notion of appresentation, then, is a kind of pairing in which possibilities of experiencing an object in its totality are conjoined, disclosing a lamp or a red ball or a house in the apperceptual event.

Husserl also employed appresentation to account for one's consciousness of another person's subjective consciousness. He conceived appresentation in this instance as an analogizing transfer to the other person of a subjectivity like one's own; thus, one infers from the apperception of the other's body a subjective consciousness like one's own (Husserl: 112–28). Edward Farley takes the main thrust of appresentation, however, to mean an intuition rather than "an act of inference from analogy," for Husserl had rejected such inference in his *Cartesian Meditations*. Husserl's concern in the Fifth Meditation was to establish the reality of the other's ego-consciousness from the transcendental givenness of the other's body; merely building up from analogy would be quite inadequate to validate such reality. Paul Ricoeur argues, however, that even Husserl was unconvinced by the argument, and Alfred Schutz explicitly rejected it (Schutz, 1962: 149; Ricoeur, 1967: 129f.). We are left, then, with a theory for which there is considerable evidence yet entailing a process of ambiguous status. Edward Farley summarizes the meaning of appresentation as follows:

> Apperception is that act in which we actually intuit components of an object which are co-present with its directly grasped facade and which are necessary to meaning or intending the object as a unity. . . . When I perceive a red ball, I do not directly intuit its interior. Therefore, the specific features of that interior remain unknown and subject to hypothesis. Do I conclude from this that there might possibly be no interior at all? Insofar as I have directly perceived by touch and sight enclosing sides, an interiorless ball is inconceivable. Although I do not in any way perceive the interior of the ball, I do intuit it as something *necessarily* co-present to the aspects which I am directly sensing, necessary to the kind of facade before me. . . . Insofar as appresentation involves grasping this a priori structure, it is more like an intuition than a hypothesis of inference. [Farley: 199f]

In this perspective, appresentation discloses another's subjectivity through the apperception of the other's body. An entity (the body) is appresenting another entity (subjectivity) of another level or "different order of reality," to use Schutz's language. One cannot confirm the existence of the other's ego-consciousness or subjectivity by any kind of originary presentation, so the other's subjectivity is a meaning that transcends sense experience.

Schutz's interpretation of symbol concerns primarily the kind of appresentation in which one experiences the other's subjectivity. Alfred Schutz considers appresentation through an entity on one level (ordinary or everyday reality) of an entity on a higher order level of reality to be the key to symbolization, as in home appresenting one's family or body appresenting the other's subjectivity. In brief, he draws out of Husserl's investigations the notion of appresentation as the process through which everyday things such as land or home or body become vehicles that mediate higher order realities such as country, family, or the other's ego-consciousness.

Although Schutz thought of appresentation as an intuition, it seems evident that appresentation of entities of a higher order or level of reality through everyday objects or situations is a figurative transference or metaphoric event of the kind I have traced in root metaphors (Schutz, 1962: 295ff.). This is to say that the appresentation of a higher order reality such as chosen people through land of promise is a metaphoric event. The duality of metaphor, literal and figurative, is precisely the event which Schutz designated appresentation. Further, as Schutz notes, the unfolding of higher levels of appresentational relations comes about through figurative transferences, as in the case of Israel's linking of kingship with the covenant, David's kingdom with the hope of restoration, messianic coming with that restoration, etc.

Schutz, we have seen, did not consider Husserl's resolution of the problem of intersubjectivity adequate and turned to symbolization as the mode of disclosure of the We-relation. To this extent, the other person's identity as person always transcends one's own consciousness. The other's Self is never given simply as an empirical entity in apperception. Self and Other are mediated to each other in symbolization. The symbolic character of selfhood is also confirmed by the historical transformations of this symbol in the Western tradition. John Dixon traces this deepening sense of inwardness in the art of the West. Similar lines of transformation can be traced in the philosophical tradition, the religious consciousness, and the political theories of the West (Heidegger, 1973; Macpherson). The Self is not a fixed, given datum of intuition. It is a symbolization which has undergone many transformations in the course of history. If the mediation of higher levels of reality such as the Self is an appresentational event and if the disclosure of the Other's ego-consciousness is paradigmatic of such an event, then appresentation is a tensive, metaphoric disclosure. Disclosures of this order cannot be subjected to tests of originary presentation as data—cannot, in other words, be reduced to apperceptual data. Tensive metaphors, as Ricoeur has argued so cogently, are not reducible to other modes of communication without violating their very nature.

The idea of symbolization enabled Schutz to break through the dualism he had created between the immediacy of the We-relation and other higher order groupings such as society and nation. However, he clung to the idea that Self and Other, I and Thou, experience an "immanent transcendence" which is of a different order from other symbolized experiences such as the nation. He put it as follows:

> i) We apprehend *individual* fellow-men and their cogitations as realities within the world of everyday life. They are within our actual or potential reach, and we share or could share with them through communication a common comprehensive environment. To be sure, we can apprehend these individual fellow-men and their cogitations only analogically through the system of appresentational references already described, and in this sense the world of the Other transcends mine; but this is an "immanent transcendence" still within the reality of our daily life. Consequently, both members of the appresentational relation through which we apprehend this transcendency belong to the same finite province of meaning, the paramount reality.
> ii) Social collectivities and institutionalized relations, however, are as such not entities within the province of meaning of everyday reality but constructs of common-sense thinking which have their reality in another subuniverse, perhaps that which

> William James called the subuniverse of ideal relations. For this very reason, we can apprehend them only symbolically; but the symbols appresenting them themselves pertain to the paramount reality and motivate our actions within it. [Schutz, 1962: 352f.]

Thus Schutz clung to the notion that the face-to-face relationship of Self and Other is of a different order from experiences of nature, society, or nation. In brief, primary groups are the kinds of relations which Schutz argued can be brought within reach as immanent encounters. This is an acceptable distinction if we recognize that these are all symbolized, higher order experiences, including that of the other person. Thus the notion of the Self as well as that of the other person is a symbolization which has been generated in history. Symbolizations on this primary level *are* subject to transformations in face-to-face experiences, and thus more amenable to change through experience than some less accessible experiences such as the nation or sacred world. However, these are matters of degree, for any symbolization may undergo transformation in experience. We may discover that a friend is betraying us. We may find that the church has failed to minister to those in need. We may find that our country has betrayed its ideals. The friend is more accessible, so I may discover the inadequacy of the friendship more readily. Many citizens, for example, found it almost impossible to believe that a president had betrayed their trust through his involvement in Watergate. Yet symbolizations are transformed by words and deeds. The tapes finally exposed the president's complicity in the coverup.

Symbolization of Self and Other is an important test case for Schutz's theory of symbols. Immanent transcendence or the presence of higher order meaning in everyday events is actually the mark of every symbolization. This is the double intentionality of symbolization which makes the symbol so ambiguous. The family is a gathering of the lives of parents and children, brothers and sisters, aunts and uncles, and many others. At the same time, the family is a particular network of bonds and everyday encounters. The family as a symbol that gathers loyalties amidst struggles bears a certain transcendence that is immanent to every aspect of family life. The appresentational event that mediates these loyalties around the home is a metaphoric disclosure that lends power and meaning to everyday relationships. Appresentation of the symbol is, in this sense, an artistic process which mediates a higher order of experience within the encounters of everyday life. Thus, artistic process proves to be fundamental to the symbolic disclosures that gather a human world of communities and higher order meanings. Where the mechanistic age seemed on the way to obliterate sensibility to higher order meanings, reducing human experience to relationships of exchange and calculation, the artistic paradigm points the way to a rediscovery of the foundations of dwelling.

Yet symbols are more than metaphoric events. Symbols reach down into the depths of life. The symbolization of the family gathers the impulses of sexuality, loyalty, care, and love in a surface meaning of interpersonal community. Surface meaning refers to accessibility rather than superficiality of meaning. Religious symbolization gathers depths of disruption and hope, trust and commitment, cosmic order and chaos, into patterns of meaning. In this respect, symbols disclose the archetypal directionalities within life and cosmos. Thus, there is a surface and depth to the symbol which is of a different order from the duality of everyday and higher order meaning. This vertical reach of the symbol can be appreciated when the appresentational event is located fully within the artistic process. Artistic process as a whole is the proper paradigm for grasping the heights and depths of symbolization.

THE ARTISTIC PARADIGM OF HUMAN DWELLING

Gadamer devoted considerable attention to the work of art as an analogue of the historical event. However, he gave little attention to the genesis of the work of art, the character of the process which he designated "transformation into structure." Gadamer took for granted that there are works of art. For his purposes, this was sufficient. Yet artistic process is a matter of first importance if it is the way that symbols come to be and, thus, the way people dwell on earth. If symbols are dynamic events of metaphoric disclosure and participation, then artistic process is of the essence of a human way of being in the world.

Few philosophers have dealt with artistic process as creatively as John Dewey. His brilliant exposition in *Art as Experience* was one of his finest works. His insights enable us to set forth a paradigm of artistic process which illumines the event of the work of art. This is the process by which the deep impulses of life and cosmos come to expression in symbol. The event of the work of art thus furnishes a model of the coming to be of symbol. The mystery of metaphor may never be grasped, since it is the mystery of creation itself. However, the inner dynamic of that metaphoric, artistic process provides a model of human dwelling, not in the narrow sense of a set of rules but in the sense of the play of human life in nature and history.

John Dewey speaks of an "esthetic-artistic process" in the coming to be of the artistic work, the interplay of esthetic sensibility and artistic creativity at each step in the emergence of the work. He links art and experience on every level of life from the simplest perception to the most exquisite artistic creations. Gadamer plays down this esthetic aspect because of his struggle against the objectification of the work of art as a merely esthetic object of appreciation. Yet esthetic sensibility is a presupposition of artistic creation as well as of participation in a work. At the same time, Dewey and Gadamer are of one mind on the involvement of audience or viewer in the artistic event. The work and the audience are engaged together in the event of the work. The work of art is, in brief, a dynamic event of creative participation, ever renewed and modified in the reproductive participation of the audience.

John Dewey's affirmation of the continuity of artistic process with all levels of human experiencing sets the stage for unfolding the dynamics of the artistic event. This sense of continuity is of great importance when one considers the artistic paradigm as a clue to human dwelling, for Dewey is arguing that art is experience raised to a higher level of intensity and enjoyed for its own sake. Experience occurs when "the material experienced runs its course to fulfillment. . . . Such an experience is a whole and carries with it its own individualizing quality and self-sufficiency" (Dewey: 35). Art for Dewey is the intensification of experience. It is not a peripheral activity confined to a precious elite. Moreover, like any full-blown experience, the artistic event is a whole in which various dimensions are interwoven. These dimensions can be identified separately by analysis, yet all of them are interwoven in the artistic event. As Dewey remarks of experience, we make the distinctions only in reflection for purposes of clarification.

Bringing forth or *letting come forth* refers to the productive dimension in the artistic event. These terms are much closer to the formulations of Paul Klee which will be explored subsequently, yet they express the intention of John Dewey's exposition. As Dewey notes, production has been so debased in modern society that we cannot use the term *production* without implying a violent process of breaking down materials and reorganizing them for our own purposes. By contrast, Dewey speaks of building up the work of art and organizing the energies ingredient to the work.

While Dewey employs the notion of expression to convey the interplay of creative process and the unfolding of the energies and potentialities of the environment, he reconceives expression in order to overcome the subjectivistic theory of art as personal expressiveness. He puts it thus:

> The real work of art is the building up of an integral experience out of the interaction of organic and environmental conditions and energies. . . . The thing expressed is wrung from the producer by the pressure exercised by objective things upon the natural impulses and tendencies—so far is expression from being the direct and immaculate issue of the latter. . . . The act of expression that constitutes a work of art is a construction in time, not an instantaneous emission. . . . It means that the expression of the self in and through a medium, constituting the work of art, is *itself* a prolonged interaction of something issuing from the self with objective conditions, a process in which both of them acquire a form and order they did not at first possess. [Dewey: 64f.]

I shall return to this point in chapter 4. It articulates the interplay of creativity and the world about us, an interplay which can be recognized as the transformation of archetypal directionalities into structure.

Another theme in the production of the work is *organization of energies*. In the bureaucratic activities of the modern world, organization has come to mean a system of control. In the arts, by contrast, one sees the authentic meaning of organization and its creative role in dwelling. Dewey formulates the issue as follows:

> The common element in all the arts, technological and useful, is organization of energy as means for producing a result. In products that strike us as merely useful, our only concern is with something beyond the thing, and if we are not interested in that ulterior product then we are indifferent to the object itself. . . . In the esthetic object the object operates—as of course one having an external use may also do—to pull together energies that have been separately occupied in dealing with many different things on different occasions, and to give them that particular rhythmic organization that we have called (when thinking of the effect and not of the mode of its effectuation), clarification, intensification, concentration. Energies that remain in a potential state with respect to one another, however actual of themselves, evoke and reenforce one another, directly for the sake of the experience that results. [Dewey: 176]

Here again Dewey is unfolding the character of artistic process as an interplay of creativity and environment in which environmental energies achieve a "particular rhythmic organization" in the work.

Forming or *re-presenting* expresses the sense of structure which we have explored in Gadamer's exposition. The material of art is drawn from nature but is appropriated in the artistic process and "so formed that it can enter into the experience of others and enable them to have more intense and more fully rounded out experiences of their own." However, in artistic process no sharp distinction holds between matter and form. Under the influence of the classical tradition, especially in its mediation by the Latin heritage, matter and form were sharply distinguished. This perspective distorted Western understanding of the relationship between the human species and nature. Artistic process restores the interplay of matter and form. *How* something is said and *what* is said are not really separable in the work of art. As Dewey puts it, the "only distinction important in art is that between matter inadequately formed and material completely and coherently formed" (Dewey: 116).

There are moments when John Dewey seems to relinquish this insight for the more traditional notion of forming matter, but this may simply be due to the irresistible weight of the metaphysical tradition which dominates Western language. My understanding, and one on which Gadamer and Dewey converge, is that natural processes are bearers of implicit directionalities or qualities which are potentially form. These are archetypal directionalities which unfold in more and less adequate ways in the symbolic, linguistic, and practical expressions of human life. In this sense, Gadamer can speak of the play of life and cosmos as self-presentation which comes to structure in artistic re-presentation. Forming or re-presenting is releasing the possibilities inherent in bios and cosmos, possibilities intrinsic to the living creature and the cosmos. Thus, interplay and forming are at one in the successful work.

The phrase *exchange of energies* expresses the play of life and cosmos as Dewey formulates it in the context of artistic process. Exchange is a reciprocity of organism and environment and of the play of life and things in the environment. With this notion, Dewey is identifying the deep structures of life which enter into the formation of symbols. He expresses it as follows:

> Interaction of environment with organism is the source, direct or indirect, of all experience and from the environment come those checks, resistances, furtherances, equilibria, which, when they meet with the energies of the organism in appropriate ways, constitute form. The first characteristic of the environing world that makes possible the existence of artistic form is rhythm. There is rhythm in nature before poetry, painting, architecture and music exist. Were it not so, rhythm as an essential property of

> form would be merely superimposed upon material, not an operation through which material effects its own culmination in experience. [Dewey: 147]

Participation by archaic peoples in these natural rhythms led to song and ritual. Art and science, *technē* in an originary sense, represented "the order of natural changes" in works and ideas. Dewey's point is that the energetics of nature are rhythmic and the formulae of these rhythms constitute our sciences and mathematics.

Dewey is not treating the artistic process in a reductionistic way. The artistic process unveils the interplay of human life with nature. John Dewey represented this struggle throughout his work yet nowhere achieved such clarity on the issue as in his work on the arts. He puts it as follows:

> "Naturalism" is often alleged to signify disregard of all values that cannot be reduced to the physical and animal. But so to conceive nature is to isolate environing conditions as the whole of nature and to exclude man from the scheme of things. [Dewey: 151f.]

The congruity of nature and the human species makes art possible. The artistic work brings to expression the archetypal rhythms of life and cosmos, releasing them into structures of experience. Artistic work raises the opaque depths to the level of meaning and experience.

Community of meaning or *celebration* expresses a fourth dimension of the artistic event. This is the continuing, cumulating, conserving, and fulfilling quality achieved in the successful work. This is a mood persisting through the totality of the artistic event, present in each of the parts, coloring the whole. Dewey argues that this quality can only be felt or experienced in a kind of intuition. Analytic reflection can extend and deepen appreciation of the event, but the sense of the whole is prior and guides the process. In the artistic event, "the resulting sense of totality is commemorative, expectant, insinuating, premonitory" (Dewey: 193). Such wholeness or unity is a mark of every experience but is raised to a higher degree of intensity in the artistic event. Hence, Dewey can accept the old formula for beauty in nature and art: unity in variety (Dewey: 161).

Reflecting on the communication of a sense of wholeness in the work, Dewey affirmed the religious or sacred quality that is mediated in the successful work:

> A work of art elicits and accentuates this quality of being a whole and of belonging to the larger, all-inclusive, whole which is the universe in which we live. This fact, I think, is the explanation of that feeling of exquisite intelligibility and clarity we have in the presence of an object that is experienced with esthetic intensity. It explains also the religious feeling that accompanies intense esthetic perception. We are, as it were, introduced into a world beyond this world which is nevertheless the deeper reality of the world in which we live in our ordinary experiences. [Dewey: 195]

The artistic event comes to fruition in this sense of totality, yet artistic consummation is present in all phases of artistic production. In artistic process, the reduction of meaning to products in the technical order is overcome, for

> the consummatory phase is recurrent throughout a work of art, and in the experience of a great work of art the points of its incidence shift in successive observations of it. This fact sets the insuperable barrier between mechanical production and use and esthetic creation and perception. In the former there are no ends until the final end is reached. Then work tends to be labor and production to be drudgery. But there is no final term in appreciation of a work of art. It carries on and is, therefore, instrumental as well as final. [Dewey: 139]

At the same time, the consummatory or fulfilling quality of the artistic event is its power of communication. As Dewey observes,

> Communication is the process of creating participation, of making common what had been isolated and singular; and part of the miracle it achieves is that, in being communicated, the convey-

> ance of meaning gives body and definiteness to the experience of the one who utters as well as to that of those who listen. [Dewey: 244]

There are, of course, many more dimensions to an artistic event which could be elaborated, but I have drawn out the four parameters or dimensions which seemed fundamental to any work. I have also followed Dewey's thought rather closely in order to do justice to his brilliant exposition and to draw out the convergence with Gadamer's notion of transformation into structure. I have, in brief, attempted with Dewey's help to spell out the event of the work of art. So far as the artistic process can serve as a root metaphor for interpreting human dwelling and the symbolization that founds it, I have made a first approximation to a paradigm of human dwelling. In figure 1: "Paradigm of the Artistic Event," the dimensions of artistic process are schematized for the sake of simplicity in presentation. The central notion of *Unity in Variety* is introduced to articulate Dewey's definition of the work of art, indicating as well the interactive character of the total process. The notion of unity in variety affirms the principle that the totality of the work respects the parts and their rhythms, releasing the archetypal rhythms of bios and cosmos into the world of experience. The unity to which this paradigm points is a harmonious interplay of parts, not a violation of the parts for the sake of mastery.[1]

SOCIALITY AND SYMBOLIZATION

The paradigm of the artistic event illumines the immanent transcendence of Self and Other which Schutz called the We-relation. The metaphoric, appresentational disclosure and the depths of symbol are diagrammed in figure 2: "Symbolization of the We-relation." In this paradigm, the dynamic process of encounter is set within the symbolic horizon of the We-relation, the unity in variety that characterizes the symbolization of Self and Other.

(A) The dimension of dialogic encounter at the base of figure 2 identifies the interplay of rhythms which we have traced in the

FIG. 1. PARADIGM OF THE ARTISTIC EVENT

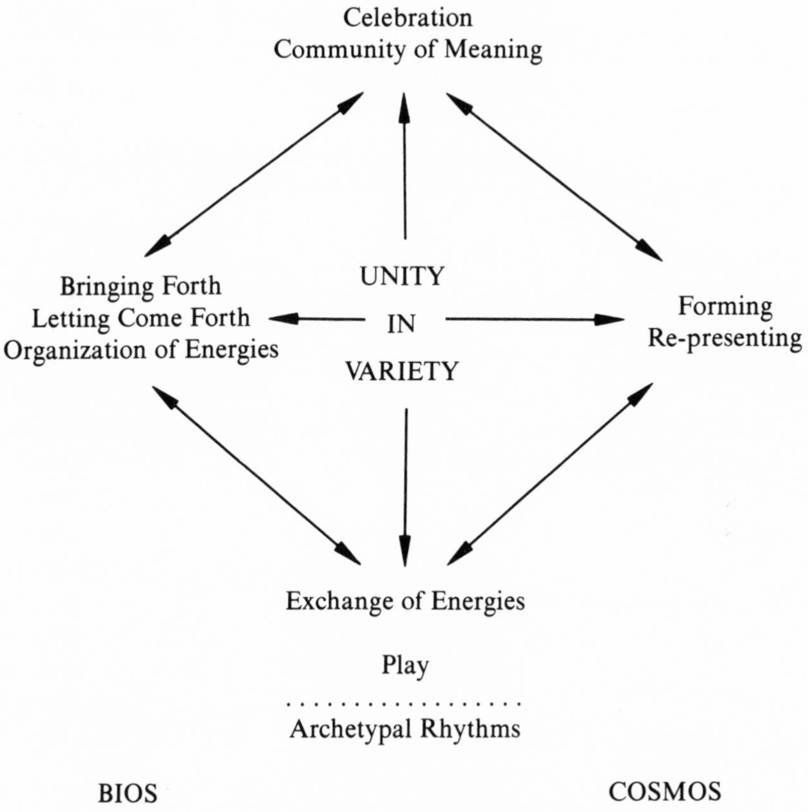

artistic process. Here conflicting and converging interests, impulses, needs, and feelings come into play. This is the deeper level of impulse and energy that constitutes the infrastructure of the appresentational event of Self and Other. No symbolization is adequate to these deeper levels of experience, so the event is a dynamic, changing and potentially creative encounter. Interpretation, as I shall trace it in chapter 3, enters creatively and transformatively into the symbolized event. It was this creative movement in the We-relation which Schutz discerned and attempted to formulate as a "tuning in" relationship (Schutz, 1964: 159–78). Such interplay can, of course, be unfolded in the event

FIG. 2. SYMBOLIZATION OF THE WE-RELATION

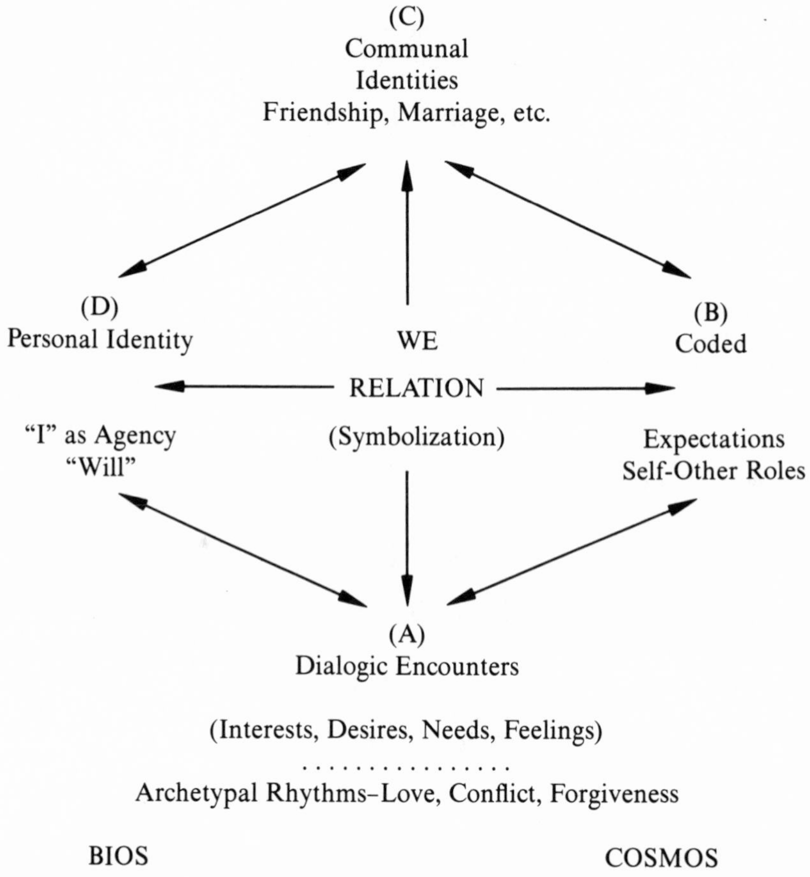

of various kinds of communities from neighborhoods to nations. Understanding a community includes, then, tracing the relevant dynamics that constitute the infrastructure of exchanges appropriate to that particular formation. The morality appropriate to such communities derives from the archetypal rhythms which they mediate. However, an interpretation of that morality requires a hermeneutic of symbols which will be considered in chapter 3.

(B) The forming or re-presenting dimension of the We-relation mediates situational aspects in coded patterns of relationship. The sociological analysis of this phenomenon is usually cast in terms of role patterning. I am suggesting that role patterning, styles of interaction, rituals of encounter and expectations of performance appresent the appropriate character of the relationship. An intimate relationship is appresented by warmth of greeting and discourse. What Schutz called typification proves to be lived interpretation in styles of action of a symbolized relationship. Hence, friendship, marriage, working relationships, and others will have appropriate modes of lived interpretation. The coding of expectations and responses, then, furnishes the situational media for appresenting the symbolized relationship. One does not expect to borrow money from one's doctor. Symbolized communities are lived through appropriate performances and attitudes.[2] A close friend may ask for the use of my car. This would be inappropriate for a stranger. On a societal level, these patterned modes of interaction take the form of laws. Particular communities generate particular orders of life. Symbolization, like any artistic event, is generated by a patterned organization of energies. These patterns or codes are metaphoric appresentations of the various communal networks in which people dwell.

(C) The appresentational mediation of pattern or form involves, as Schutz indicates, at least two provinces of meaning—everyday affairs and one or more higher order levels of meaning. In the case of Self and Other, a We-relation, these higher order realms are indicated by communal identities such as friendship and marriage. These are mundane symbolizations in the sense that they are experienced within the everyday world, even though they constitute totalities which transcend apperceptual givenness. The symbolization of Self and Other mediates a higher order meaning in the Western heritage and perhaps in all cultures. This higher order mediation is ambiguous and invites interpretation and transformation in societal process. The shifting patterns of male and female relationships in our period would be exemplary of this historical process.

There are also higher order symbolizations which transcend the mundane realm—scientific, oneiric, religious, philosophical, and other realms. These symbolizations also involve mediations within the everyday realm, synthesizing two or more orders of reality; however, they exceed our grasp and require translation and interpretation in the mundane realm. Philip Wheelwright's distinction between steno-symbols and depth symbols discriminates among these transcending symbolizations. He draws on I. A. Richards's proposal that meaning or meaningful situation involves two aspects: "what means and what is meant, a semantic carrier and a semantic content, or . . . *vehicle* and *tenor,* V and T" (Wheelwright, 1968: 7). Steno-symbols are deliberately developed to assure clarity and consistency in discourse. They are conventional. Steno-symbols and corresponding modes of discourse develop in sciences, logics, technical fields such as medicine and law, and generally where precision is at stake. In these realms, the V-T relation is kept stable by fiat in order to achieve consistent communication and understanding. For example, *home* will be stripped of its rich connotations and taken to denote a place of residence. By contrast, the V-T relation in depth symbols

> is developed and modulated by the creative and discriminating activity of man, in his human capacity as the being who can apprehend and express meanings through language. His materials are drawn from his experiences, from his imaginative expansions of experience, and from various kinds of psychic association, some of which may have erupted unaccountably from the depths of his unconscious. [Wheelwright, 1968: 13]

Thus, in a depth symbol, home mediates a sense of belonging, nurture, and security. It is obvious that these basic modes of symbolization involve different problems of interpretation and varying truth-claims, issues which we shall explore in chapter 3. However, both steno-symbolizations and depth symbolizations involve transcending structures and both, in their own ways, mediate meaningful realms of experience. In general, steno-symbols mediate objectified meanings which Owen Barfield called realms of alpha-thinking (Barfield: chap. 8) and Martin Heidegger called the world present-at-hand (*vorhanden*) (Heidegger, 1962: 128ff.). By contrast, depth symbols mediate realms of otherness or what Wheelwright sometimes refers to as paralogical meanings, where logical refers to the structure of steno-discourse. The suppression of symbols in a mechanistic age can be understood as the attempt to reduce all expressive, depth symbols to steno-discourse; in other words, symbols such as land or home are reduced to a piece of property or place of residence, discarding the richer meanings or treating them simply as disease of language. I shall return to this issue in chapter 4 when the clash of traditional and technological worlds is fully explored. The technological world imposes its calculating rationality on traditional peoples, charging them with irrationality and claiming a monopoly on rational understanding.

(D) Self and Other are, then, symbolizations that develop within the matrix of higher order meanings such as family, friendship, and intimate community. However, these face-to-face relationships have a special character that emerges in the artistic agency of letting come forth or bringing forth. This is identified as personal identity in figure 2, for it has to do with the struggle of the person to unfold his or her own possibilities of being in the context of symbolizations of selfhood and corresponding patterns of expectation. The acting *I* never gains access to its being as *I* except in reflection anymore than we can see through our eyes in their seeing. Yet the *I* as agency or will is a transcending interpreter who is never reducible to mere object. Where symbol and patterning are appropriate to emerging possibilities of personhood (archetypal rhythms of life), identities and role-structures can be harmonized. Where the fit is felt as inadequate, as, for example, in feminine roles in modern society, and where conditions open possibilities of transformation, desymbolization and resymbolization can occur through innovative interpretations. Dialogical communities furnish a crucial, relational structure for such transformations, though ultimately the transforming interpretation has to alter the institutional networks in community, work, politics, and other realms of activity. The special character of the face-to-face relationship derives from the self-transcending power of personhood, the otherness of the I, which generates tensions and dynamic transformations in life. The being of a people, as we shall see, is also such a transcending power of historical transformation. This is the locus of the liberating power of human creativity which is central to the root metaphor of artistic process.

The paradigm of artistic process drawn in figure 2 offers some clues to the relationship of men and women in a more humane and just society. The paradigm is misleading in one respect, since it suggests a harmonious unfolding of human relationships through dialogue. However, the baseline of the figure identifies rhythms of love, conflict and forgiveness. This baseline points to a process of creation that I shall delineate more fully in chapter 4. However, the interplay of feelings, desires, needs, and interests reveals a dialogue that breeds conflict, misunderstanding, negations, and challenges. The rhythms of nature and human life may eventuate in harmonies but they manifest themselves in contention. It is no accident that one of the primordial forms of play to which Huizinga alludes is the agonistic struggle of the contest. Conflict and challenge are not debasing forces of human dwelling, so long as they do not explode in violence. Conflict is of the essence of all creativity. Only in the challenge of what is lacking in experience or oppressive to life are creative powers released.

The twentieth century has seen the challenge of the women's struggle for liberation against the oppressive forces that have for so long relegated women to a subservient role. This is the opening of what Beverly Harrison refers to as "the longest revolution." The challenge to male domination goes back perhaps as long as history and had significant manifestations in the nineteenth century. It now seems to be moving irresistibly to overcome ancient injustices, breaking open the way to mutuality of respect in work and politics, education and religious life. There are, as was noted earlier, powerful forces of resistance, attempting to restore the organic hierarchy of being that rationalized the servitude of women throughout Western history. The foundations of this organicist heritage have eroded, however, for that metaphysical order of form and matter no longer makes sense in biological or human life. Evolutionary theory demonstrated long ago that life is not a matter of fixed forms but a process of coding and recoding in changing patterns of life.

The artistic process points to a mutuality of Self and Other, men and women, women and women, parents and children, men and men, in which equality of humanity is the keynote. The artistic process is a human process to which all persons are summoned, taking over the precious gifts of life with which they are nurtured and contributing creatively to the enlargement of those gifts. Foundational to such an understanding of mutual love is the symbol of creation which I shall connect with the artistic vision in chapter 4. Nevertheless, the patterning of roles, structuring of institutions, formation of communal identities and opportunities for expression of personal identities—all of these dimensions of the artistic process—are to be tested by appropriateness to this dialogue of mutuality and equality (Durka and Smith: chap. 7).

SYMBOL AS WORK OF ART

John Dewey's interpretation of artistic process reveals the deep structure as well as metaphoric disclosure of symbolic events. Symbols like works of art are dynamic events that live in the day to day operations of persons and institutions. A people's dwelling is the unfolding of the power and vision of symbols, even as the audience is the fourth wall of the drama. However, to say that artistic process is a root metaphor of human dwelling does not mean that dwelling is a work of art in the proper sense. Dwelling is neither painting nor composing. Human dwelling rests upon symbolic foundations (in a dynamic, historical sense) from which various modes of interpretation are generated. To say that the human species dwells artistically upon the earth is a metaphoric notion.

Nevertheless, Alfred Schutz's proposal that symbols are generated through appresentation underscores the artistic character of symbols. Appresentation is a metaphoric, poetic process according to the preceding interpretation. By the same token, artistic process is an appresentational, metaphoric event of disclosure. In this sense, symbols and works of art have a common origin and dynamic structure. Nevertheless, works of art and symbols are different, as Gadamer observes (Gadamer: 136f.). The arts of painting and sculpture are free and unbound in comparison with symbols, for symbols are deeply rooted in the archetypal rhythms of life and cosmos. The arts proper move freely on the creative edge of history though they draw upon these deeper impulses of the cosmos. Symbols plumb the depths of life and nature, gathering the impulses and rhythms which give direction to the cosmos. Artistic process and symbolization differ, then, in the degree to which they are bound and free (Ricoeur, 1976: 57–63).

Yet Hans-Georg Gadamer draws a more profound distinction between work of art and symbol than the one we acknowledge between degrees of freedom. His ontology of the painting suggests that the symbol merely "represents" while the painting is an increase of being of the original. It is certainly true that God is not more fully God in being symbolized. Nevertheless, the sharpness of this distinction between work of art and symbol has to be taken with reservation. The cosmic symbolization of the divine life in the rising and setting of the sun is radically different from symbolization in the "historical" events of the Exodus or the Cross. In one sense, anything can be transformed into symbol through hierophany, as Mircea Eliade claims. Yet symbols are particular. Their disclosures are intimately bound up with the vehicles which they transform in appresentational disclosures, even as material and form are inseparable in artistic works. The Cross puts an indelible stamp on the disclosure of divinity in the Christian heritage. The symbol says what it says in the way that it re-presents higher orders of meaning in particular, everyday things and events. In religious symbols, the divine life is revealed in its being through particular symbolizations. To speak of divinity as more or other in being than its disclosure in symbolic manifestation affirms the otherness of the mystery. Faith recognizes that the sacred mystery is never exhausted in a particular symbolization. Yet the divine life is not a reality separate from the disclosure events in which the mystery reveals itself. Indeed, the divine life is more fully itself in the disclosure events of Exodus and Cross through which the mystery reveals the power of liberating love for the world. This is the point at which Gadamer's idealistic inclination diverts his attention from the centrality of symbol (Gadamer: 363, 395).

A word of caution is appropriate at this point. The symbol is ambiguous and, indeed, conceals as well as discloses the powers and rhythms of life and cosmos which it mediates. To identify the symbol wholly with the higher order reality it mediates is to reify that which transcends. This leads to idolatry of the nation or family or sacred revelation. When the mediation of higher order realities supplants the reality, symbolization becomes idolatry. The people cried, "The Temple! The Temple!" trusting that Jahweh would not desert the temple despite their unfaithfulness, but the prophet pointed to the illusion in their cry. Similarly the techno-scientific age has treated the symbolization of natural entities, the empirical things which it investigates, as the final and ultimate realities, the touchstone of truth (Barfield: 110f.). This reification of the higher order realities that are mediated in symbolization is the peculiar idolatry of the modern age. To this idolatry, as to the idolatry of ancient times, one can only say that the symbol discloses ambiguously, never exhausting the transcending power and depth of that which it mediates. But these considerations have already shifted the focus of consideration to the problem of living and interpreting the symbols that found human dwelling.

NOTES

1. The author is indebted to J. Ronald Engel for introducing the work of John Dewey into mutual discussions of the central place of artistic process in human dwelling. Dr. Engel has extended Dewey's interpretation to a whole range of considerations in his volume *Sacred Sands* (Middletown, Conn.: Wesleyan University Press, forthcoming). Nevertheless, we share a common task in unfolding the power of the artistic metaphor for the liberation of nature and life in a mechanistic age.

2. Erving Goffman is one of the few social scientists who has investigated the performatory character of the networks of human relationship that constitute statuses and roles; see his classic study *Asylums*.

3

SYMBOL AND INTERPRETATION

PEOPLE dwell on earth symbolically through work, love, suffering, deciding, celebrating, and struggling. Even in its moments of tedium human life is a dynamic process, its activities coded or patterned in networks of interpersonal relations, forms of cultural expression and systems of motivation. Love is expressed in familial and personal networks. Work is carried on in shops and offices, schools and plants, farms and research laboratories. Deciding occurs in markets, shopping malls, offices, legislatures, and courts. Some actions are spontaneous but most are organized around expectations. The foreman and the operator know within limits what is expected on each side. And this coding includes appropriate kinds of language, attitudes, and styles of conduct.

The activities, attitudes, and patterns of daily life unfold the symbols that found our world. Sometimes parental conduct embodies the role of adults in family life, symbolizing the family concretely. At other times, as in child abuse or incest, parental actions subvert traditional symbols of the family. Cultural expressions may explicate symbolizations of life and cosmos; they may also subject such symbols to radical critique and transformation. Galileo's questions about the traditional cosmic symbolism led to church censorship. Patterns of working and merchandising also unfold a symbolized order of production and consumption, sometimes transforming that order, as in the shift from craft to factory production. The everyday world is an interpretative process that lives out and alters the symbolizations of a people's world. Interpretation is, in this sense, a lived process of symbolic enactment. Interpretation is only secondarily a reflective process.

Three principles guide this development of the meaning of interpretation. (1) A symbolized world not only invites but requires interpretation. (2) Dwelling is linguistic through and through, and thus *lived interpretation* is an unfolding of discourse. (3) Reflective interpretations such as this essay and all social and ethical inquiries are second degree interpretations which lift into view lived interpretations. The second principle, the linguisticality of human dwelling, requires clarification. The term *interpretation* tends to divert attention from the concrete nexus of socioeconomic struggles and may thus seem to be devoid of the element of praxis.[1] However, lived interpretation involves all regions of discourse from arts and letters to work and construction.

Lived interpretation in thought, action, mood, decision, technical process, and creative production is generated through language. A despondent mood may be difficult to express in words when a friend asks how we feel, but even our experience of that mood depends upon a linguistic identification. At times we sense something stirring in the depths of our being which cannot be put into words. After a period of time we may realize what troubled us, and we have a sense of "knowing" what it was all about. Such simple actions as opening a door and leaving a room depend upon linguistic powers that bring those possibilities within our reach. Through language I am already within the opening of the door as I entertain the possibility of leaving the room. Language is no mere tool with which we manipulate the world around us. Language constitutes the possibilities of being in that world while transcending it toward new possibilities. In an unbearable situation we may imagine other situations and possibilities. Language is more than a tool; it is our way of being in the world as working, loving, fearing, enjoying, and hoping.

Lived interpretation is, thus, impregnated with language, even though some modes of interpretation involve actions such as walking and dispositions such as fearing that seem to be protolinguistic. Lived interpretation is embodied, enacted, and expressed discourse. Lived interpretation is language come to life in works of art, patterns of action and motivational dispositions. Language is the historical concreteness of symbols. Symbols constitute the regions and horizons of language.

HISTORY AS SYMBOL/INTERPRETATION

Symbol and interpretation interact in dynamic historical events. The term *language* conceals this reality, for language refers to a coded system whereas living language becomes concrete in discourse, speech-events, conversations, broadcasts, and publications. In the everyday world of speaking and hearing, writing and reading, understanding and misunderstanding, a people's language lives. Hence, the proper linguistic perspective on interpretation is discourse. Language is the crystallization of discourse at a particular point in time. The slow changes through which languages develop come about through living discourse. Like everything else in human dwelling, languages have histories, for they have a past that shapes their present and a future that is still unfolding.

Symbols also have histories. They unfold and change over time. But to say this understates the historicality of symbols. It is more appropriate to say that people dwell historically because they dwell symbolically. Symbols mediate the continuity of past and future so that dwelling achieves permanence amidst changing, lived interpretations. The symbolization of nature in the Western world is a striking instance of continuity and change. Science and technology altered the interpretation of nature, yet the Western experience of nature persisted through a shared symbolization. The changes in symbolizations such as polity and economy came more slowly, altering patterns of life a little at a time.

Symbols are unpacked through lived interpretations, while retaining their power to gather a world of meanings within a shared horizon. This phenomenon of continuity and change is analogous to the experience of a work of art. A drama like *King*

Lear, for example, is reenacted in changing contexts. The original meaning of the drama persists as a tragedy of evil and chaos amidst the appearances of good (Spencer: 135f.). Yet each interpretative reenactment brings out new dimensions appropriate to changing historical contexts. Some aspects vital to earlier performances may fade into the background while new depths and insights are disclosed. An authentic reenactment does not try to reproduce the life and setting of sixteenth-century England, but unfolds the drama within the horizon constituted by its whole history. There is, to be sure, an originary dramatic work which says something particular, but the meaning of what is said is a dynamic, unfolding event that is enriched in each reproduction. Works of art, and symbols as well, are dynamic structures which are lived in their interpretations, not static structures to be cloned.

Symbol and interpretation interplay reciprocally in this dynamic process of enactment that we call dwelling. There is no symbol without interpretation and, indeed, there is no access to symbol except through interpretation. By the same token, interpretations arise from and are oriented toward horizons constituted by symbolizations. Scientific inquiries into nature arose within a horizon of possibilities and gradually transformed that symbolic horizon. This interplay of symbol/interpretation constitutes the historical event of dwelling. Dwelling is historical, bearing its past into a future, because it is mediated and gathered through symbolizations. Human consciousness could not constitute an historical identity, for consciousness is an inner, temporal flow which gains its bearings through language, places, relationships, and events.[2]

Self and other, as we noted, are symbolic events (see fig. 2, chap. 2), and like all symbolizations they are historical. To say that human selves come to be in birth, mature, and pass away is a superficial statement of the temporality of the self. In this objective view of temporality, selves are in motion or change, and those changes can be measured in linear time from beginning to middle to end. By the same token, Arnold Toynbee devoted his major work to tracing the origins, development, and decay of great civilizations, an account which was, of course, more than a necrology, for Toynbee sought to discern the inner dynamics of creativity and degradation in these cultures. A superficial view of temporality would merely chronicle this coming to be and passing away, treating civilizations as though they were *in* time rather than temporal in their very constitution.

The temporality of dwelling and symbol is more deeply rooted than linear change or motion; in fact, the possibility of discerning change or motion presupposes this more radical temporality of the symbolized world. A story or biography or written history presupposes a radical temporality of dwelling, for such events depend upon a unity of past, present, and future which no linear, spatialized time can yield. Even the notion of self-fulfillment presupposes a more radical temporality than mere flux, for fulfillment implies completion or wholeness to the temporal process in which the past comes to fruition in a future consummation. This radical temporality is mediated by the symbolization of the life world in which we dwell.

The symbol of the self is a helpful clue to radical temporality, since the self achieves some sense of identity through an interplay of the past with a vivid present in the light of an open future. We get a sense of radical temporality by considering pastness, presentness, and futurity in isolation before attempting to describe the unity in which we experience these moments.

The pastness of a mature self is more than an infancy, childhood, and adolescence which is over and done. The early years are a continuing reality in the self's identity, filling the present with images, fears, expectations, scenarios to be repeated or avoided, and hopes to be cherished. These scenarios are lived interpretations of the symbol of the self. Selfhood gathers its pastness into its identity, working and reworking lived interpretations in the past in the context of the present. This is one of the profound insights and working principles of psychotherapy. The symbolization of the self is not fixed once and for all but is ever being reworked. In mental illness the self may be fixated at a certain point in earlier symbolization, making the past not a creative power but a dead hand that cripples the present. The presentness of the past in its distortions and disclosures obtains for all symbolizations in human dwelling.

Decisive events like the Exodus project the possibilities of the present for Israel, shaping the future in many different ways. A people's history is constituted by such crucial events, lived interpretations which forge the symbolization of their identity. American identity, for example, was constituted by certain events such as the encounter with wilderness, the Puritan Covenant, the enslavement of Indians and black people, the Revolution and the Civil War. These are not merely past events. They are constitutive of the American present. Slavery and its consequences in segregation, Jim Crow and urban ghettoization continue to corrupt American life. Pastness interplays with presentness in a dynamic way, sometimes contributing creatively to the present, sometimes weighing down the present with unresolved distortions. The symbolization of a people's identity gathers these events, holding them open for new interpretation and transformation.

Futurity has a special privilege in human dwelling, conjoining with presentness to liberate people from the weight of the past. Even in a superficial sense, one is aware of the privilege of futurity through planning and projects. However, futurity enters into the present in an even more radical sense. A linguistic species not only has a future but is its future, as possibilities. The symbol of the self is again a vivid indicator of the power of futurity. Whatever the possibilities of one's future, the unavoidable possibility is death. Death is not simply an event that will happen to a person someday. Death is integral to the everyday activity of waking and sleeping, thinking and feeling, loving and hating. Existentialist philosophy has given much attention to this radical interplay of our being as unto death with the presentness of our decisions and projects. In attending to the symbolization of the self, existentialist thought has unfolded this special power of futurity to shape the present. The radical futurity of not-being may, of course, be mediated in the symbolization of a people rather than the selfhood of the individual. Native Americans, at least in their more traditional dwelling, encounter the anxiety of mortality, the radical futurity of not being anymore, in the symbolization of the tribe or people. Individual death is, to be sure, a painful and difficult experience, but the radical threat is to the people—threatened by starvation, disease, warfare, or genocide by white settlers (Deloria: chap. 10). Futurity is, of course, more than mortality, for it harbors possibilities of renewal, transcendence of past distortions, and hope of completion. In this respect, a people dwells within the horizon of radical futurity, a futurity that is mediated in symbols of promise, whether this be a promise of the return of the rising sun, an assurance of rains to renew the arid soil, or trust in the Shalom for which the people longs.

The radical temporality mediated in symbols is perhaps most evident in the present of a self or people. A superficial present is a vanishing point on a moving line, disappearing even as it appears. The radical present is more than this. It is well exemplified by a linguistic expression like, "Many guests were present" (Heidegger, 1972: 10ff.). We also use the expression, "A person of considerable presence." Both of these expressions refer to the weight of presentness that is gathered around an occasion or a person. Presentness, then, is a moment when our world comes together, drawing everything present under its sway. Presentness is a centering or gathering that creates a special quality in an event. The guests are present. They lend their presence to the occasion; at the same time, the occasion gathers the guests and creates a special quality of their gathering. In Yeats's much quoted expression about the dissolution of the modern world, "The center does not hold," one can recognize the radical temporality of presentness, for the "center" is the spatial and temporal event of symbol that gathers a people into a shared present. By contrast, if dwelling is reduced to techniques and interests, the shared world of a people erodes. The centering of human dwelling is strangely temporal. It depends upon the symbols that gather a world and bind a people into a public. When the center weakens, personal life is fragmented, individuals pursue their own interests, and the public happiness deteriorates.

The rich present that gathers is the radical moment in which a self or a people achieves a sense of wholeness, a sense of freedom to act in concert—thinking, deciding, and celebrating as one people. We say, "The guests were present for the marriage of Susan and Peter," and we know already that they shared a special presence in virtue of the occasion. When Martin Luther King, Jr., appeared at the head of a march during the civil rights struggle, people gathered as though drawn by a magnetic force—ready, hopeful, expectant. Freedom to act, decide, choose, or transcend conditioning limitations is a gift of radical presence, a present opening upon a shared future. Centering is mediated by the symbolization of a people's identity; thus, symbols enspace as well as temporalize the world. The center is energized by the rituals and deeds of public life. Presence is a gift of freedom to overcome distortions of the past in the light of new possibilities for a fuller life.

Radical presentness is, thus, a nexus of past and future in which possibilities emerge for decision. In this sense, creative interpretation depends upon radical temporality in which pastness can be critically transformed in the light of an open future. The symbol mediates the horizon of that futurity even as it bears the richness of the past. The symbolization of nature in the Renaissance held open a horizon of inquiry that no ecclesiastical authority could close. It also gathered a long tradition of inquiries and reflections that led and misled the speculations of the astronomers. The symbolization of nature and cosmos mediated those possibilities. Creative interpretation that challenged the geocentric astronomy appropriated those possibilities in a new science and technology.

The historicality of human dwelling, its continuity amidst change, is thus mediated by the radical temporality of symbol. Symbols bear pastness. Symbols project futurity. Symbols create a present by gathering a world, opening a time-space for creative action. A self is not a finished symbolization of human being but a bearer of possibilities. The same holds for a people or a family or a neighborhood. What, then, does one mean by the symbolization of a people? Certainly a people is constituted by the symbolizations of its origin and the events that shaped its history. But a people is also a symbolization of possibilities of completion. This is the privilege of futurity in human dwelling. We are an unfinished species, unfinished peoples. We dwell in anticipation just as we wrestle with the weight of the past. But a people is a diverse multiplicity, stratified in social classes, distributed in regional as well as ethnic groups. Who, then, is the bearer of a people's future? It would seem that the social class or segment that represents the future and struggles for that future truly re-presents the authentic reality of the people. Those sectors of life bearing that promise of a future are, then, the creative interpreters of a people's identity. Biblical prophecy and narrative saw the poor of the earth as bearer of the covenant promise. The poor are, in this sense, creative interpreters of Israel's identity. Liberation theologies look to the poor and oppressed who struggle for justice as the representative of the people. The proletariat, a crucial symbol in Marxism, is similarly a bearer of the future. In this sense, interpretation of a people's identity has a normative character; it is morally and spiritually qualified. A people's history mediates as yet unrealized hopes for freedom and justice. Symbolizations are not neutral or value-free. They are bearers of possibilities of completion and consummation. A people lives in its possibilities even as it struggles with its present problems. Routinization or mechanical repetition fixes lived interpretations in past patterns, preserving an order that perpetuates the power of oppressors. Creative interpretations gather a future that transcends past oppressions, fulfilling the authentic promise of the past. Such creative interpretations are borne by those who hunger for justice and peace, even though they may be voiced by prophets who speak for that future.

Lived interpretation contributes to continuity as well as change in human dwelling. Patterns of familial relationship, friendship, religious life, and political organization manifest remarkable continuities over time. In fact, lived interpretation is so stable in most societies that the human sciences have obscured the integrative power of symbols and settled for "behavioral patterning" as the medium of continuity. This is not an either/or situation. Symbols gather and sustain a world. Lived interpretations embody and unfold that world. The Nazi movement, for example, drew upon the power of the symbolization of a Germanic people and culture. However, it distorted the promise of universal culture for the sake of domination. The

Third Reich disfigured its authentic promise in a lived interpretation of terror and violence.

Mircea Eliade has observed that symbols tend toward system (Eliade, 1958: 449f.). Religious, political, moral, economic, and other symbolizations tend toward coherence. By contrast, lived interpretations in these various spheres of dwelling tend to lose coherence, at least this is the case in a modern, complex society. Family life becomes segregated from economic activity. Religious life develops its own private style and values. Moral practices are distributed over different spheres in such a way that good practice in business would be quite unacceptable in a family or neighborhood. At the same time, symbols furnish coherence even amidst such a pluralization of lived interpretations. In fact, encompassing symbols of the modern world such as the market and the cash nexus permeate all realms of life including the most intimate relationships of sexuality and personal community. This implicit coherence only comes to light as reflection lets the higher orders of meaning show forth from lived interpretations. Symbolizations and the root metaphors that furnish clues to them provide whatever coherence a people experiences. At the same time, moral and social scientific inquiries tend to treat polity and economy, family and bureaucracy, sexuality and industry as discrete, segregated realms. Thus, moral and social scientific inquiries accentuate the incoherence of the modern world, concealing its deeper unity.

Reflective interpretations in science, ethics, or any other field can thus create a spurious incoherence unless they are raised to the level of the symbolizations that organize the world. Symbols gather and order the world. Although interpretations may challenge that order and often do, they distance themselves from that world only to return to it. It is this interplay of symbol/interpretation which constitutes the historicality of human dwelling—arising from originary symbolizations in pastness that undergo change and even transformation through lived interpretations in the light of a beckoning future. Human dwelling is historical because it arises in symbolization and unfolds within the temporal and spatial horizons which symbols mediate. Human dwelling is dynamic and changing because it is lived through interpretations that are always reaching toward new possibilities within symbolic horizons, sometimes in disfiguring distortions, at other times in creative transformations.

LIVED INTERPRETATION AS "TEXT"

Lived interpretation is linguistic as its core. Like all linguistic events the creative dynamic of lived interpretation is metaphor (Wheelwright, 1962: chap. 3). Language arises in a metaphoric process and unfolds through the creative movement of metaphoric innovation. This is the fundamental analogy between lived interpretation and artistic process that guides our inquiry into the nature of lived interpretations. Such interpretations are inscribed in the hearts and lives of people, in their patterns of family relationships and in the various networks which organize their activities. Lived interpretations are much more like written texts than like transitory conversations. They are inscribed on the human scene like the grammatical coding of a written text. Paul Ricoeur has analyzed the unique significance of the written text, especially as it bears on problems of interpretation (Ricoeur, 1976: chap. 2). One may recall a conversation with a friend. The *said* of the conversation has a certain stability in time. It can be remembered, though the details may fade from memory. Weeks later, meeting the friend, that conversation may be recalled. What was *said* in the encounter is remembered and reviewed. Ricoeur refers to this *said* of the speech-event as the precipitate of discourse which gains stability and objectivity of a special kind in the written text. The written text, unlike a conversation, becomes independent of the author, transcending his or her intentions as it enters the public world. The audience of discourse is also transformed by the written text, for the said of the text is open to anyone who can read. One does not have to be a partner to the conversation in order to share in the communication of the text. Independence of the author and generalization of the audience make the text vulnerable to a variety of interpretations. One cannot ask of the text, as one might in a conversation, "What did you mean by that remark?" Understanding now depends upon how one interprets the text.

The written text as a work of art is a useful analogue to the lived interpretations of human dwelling. Lived interpretations are coded like texts. The discourse that underlies lived interpretation achieves objective continuity like a text in patterns of human dwelling. Parental roles, for example, are shared widely among social groups, cutting across social class and other barriers. There are, of course, differences in the particular enactments of parental roles among different groups but, within a society that shares a common symbolization of family life, being a father or mother is defined by a shared pattern of expectations. Individuals may deviate rather sharply from that pattern, but friends or neighbors may well remark that he or she is not a "good" parent. *Good* here usually means living up to the norms that code the lived interpretation of parenthood. These are practical, moral, and religious codings of what it means to hold a particular position within the network of familial relationships. They are practical codings in that they tend to stabilize family life. They are moral, for breaking them usually leads to moral censure. They are religious in the broad, nonconfessional sense of reflecting the way in which a people believes life should be ordered. Under conditions of change, any or all of these aspects may be challenged.

Paul Ricoeur distinguishes analytically between the message of the text and its coding in order to avoid reducing the meaning of the text to the sense that is mediated in its grammatical structure. For example, a narrative recounts events in a descriptive form; the narrator interprets, to be sure, but strives to let the events tell themselves (Ricoeur, 1980: 77). By contrast, the story or folk tale annihilates everyday events in order to redescribe reality and open new possibilities of meaning (Ricoeur, 1980: 100ff.). In similar fashion, the coding of various genres can be identified and the immanent sense can be recognized. This is the way in which Ricoeur interprets the term *genre* and the formal *sense* it mediates. In Ricoeur's words:

> The generative devices, which we call literary genres, are the technical rules presiding over their production. And the style of a work is nothing else than the individual configuration of a singular

> product or work. . . . With literature the problems of inscription and production tend to overlap. The same may be said for the concept of text, which combines the condition of inscription with the texture proper to the works generated by the productive rules of literary composition. Text means discourse both as inscribed and wrought. [Ricoeur, 1980: 33]

The genre has its particular sense as a grammatical structure, the poem creating a mood, the story redescribing an aspect of the world, the parable bursting the expectations that govern everyday activity. This can be called the immanent sense or directionality of a text. Sense or immanent meaning is formal and universal to all texts of a particular genre in whatever time, place, or cultural epoch. Ricoeur urges that this immanent sense be treated in unity with the kind of world that the text projects, what he calls its "referential sense." Thus, the parable has its internal structure that belongs universally to the genre, but a particular parable also says something specific about our world and its possibilities. In the work of art, as John Dewey made clear, the inner, formal structure and the substance or referential sense belong together. How something is re-presented and what is re-presented belong intimately together in the successful work. Thus, in reading the text a world is disclosed that reconstitutes our world. As Ricoeur puts it, "Our world is given to us through the ensemble of references opened up by every kind of text, descriptive or poetic, that I have read, understood and loved" (Ricoeur, 1976: 36ff.). This emphasis on the way a text refers to and projects a world of meaning opens out upon the world of symbol, clarifying the way in which lived interpretations operate as inscriptions of symbol and disclosures of symbol.

Taking the text as analogue to the inscription of symbol in lived interpretation, the most obvious mode of inscription is *cultural expression*. Such expression occurs in literature, the sciences, philosophy and theology, and generally in the arts and humanities. This cultural mode of lived interpretation is closest to the text proper, for culture in this restricted sense produces texts or works. The cultural mode of inscription is likewise relatively accessible to understanding, for arts, humanities, and sciences intend to communicate and to be understood or appreciated. Generally, cultural inscriptions integrate message and coding in such a way that they say what they say in the way that they are. The quality of the experience that a work of art generates is brought into being by the organization of energies in certain rhythms. This coding of energies conveys an immanent sense and mediates a projection of world or referential sense. Cultural expressions are lived interpretations that empower participation in a symbolic world and/or restructure those symbols, releasing hidden possibilities for transformation. Religious, political, and scientific expressions may sustain a common world through rituals, proclamations, and textbook inquiries. On the other hand, a prophet's speech may redefine a religious situation; a Gettysburg Address may reinterpret a people's struggle; a theory of relativity may project a new paradigm of the physical universe. Cultural expressions may be creative interpretations as well as confirmations of a symbolic legacy. In different ways, they empower participation in the symbolized world that constitutes a people's identity.

Patterning of action or praxis is a somewhat different, though interrelated, mode of inscription of symbol in lived interpretation. Praxis may be innovative as well as stabilizing in dwelling, though institutionalized praxis tends to be more traditional than cultural expression. Patterns of action are always more difficult to change than cultural interpretations, because praxis organizes the routines of ordinary life, lending stability to the networks of relationships in which people manage from day to day. Routines of working and relaxing, teaching and learning, playing and celebrating, buying and selling, building and repairing, these and many other patterns preserve a system of expectations through which people can anticipate their future. Disruption of such routines can be very disturbing. Loss of a job or divorce in a family breaks routine as well as damages a whole network of relationships. The world of praxis is, in fact, remarkably stable, yet it embodies a network that can easily be dislocated when a single tie is broken or disrupted.

Institutionalized praxis is also more difficult to read or interpret than cultural expressions. The immanent sense or meaning of institutional praxis can be interpreted, to be sure, as has been demonstrated by the human sciences. This is especially true when comparative methods are used to consider the formal structure of kinship systems, economies, polities, religious patterns, or educational practices. Similarities and differences can be isolated and formal patterns can be identified. There are, of course, differences among social scientists in their interpretations of these patterns of action according to the perspectives which they project, but certain general categories of kinship, economic exchange, polity, etc., have emerged and constitute a common world of social scientific discourse (Winter, 1966: chap. 6). However, the symbolic world projected in praxis is not so readily accessible to social scientific interpretation. There is an opacity to praxis which makes it difficult to read as lived interpretation. In those instances where social scientists attempt to read the symbols that are enacted in praxis, they usually depend upon cultural expressions to provide the clues to the projected world. Thus, studies of classical Greece and Rome have drawn upon the arts and humanities to provide interpretations of the praxis of the classical world, reading the praxis in relation to the culture. The same has been true until very recently of biblical studies which have been, for the most part, cultural rather than institutional inquiries. This is a defensible method of inquiry but runs the danger of obscuring the dialectical tensions between praxis and cultural expression. Cultural expressions are more amenable to manipulation, even falsification, than institutional praxis. Praxis is the way in which a people "says" its world through its life and action. How a society treats its environment, cares for or neglects its poor, educates its young, copes with mortality, and endures its sufferings says very concretely the kind of symbolic world in which it dwells. There is every reason to explore lived interpretations through the interplay of cultural and institutional modes of expression. There is also reason to suspect a total reliance upon cultural expressions which are usually the preserve of cultural elites.

Motivational inscriptions of symbol are more rigorously coded than cultural expressions or institutional praxis. The attitudes, interests, expectations, and idealized images of human personality are internalized through familial experiences, peer group exchanges, educational processes, rites of passage, and other experiences. Some social theorists draw a parallel between motivational coding and the genetic coding of instinctual processes, but this biological analogy attributes more stability to motivational coding than is warranted from the evidence of personal transformations (Geertz: 216ff.). Scenarios in the early years shape motivations which persist throughout our lives but they can be rewritten, especially under the impact of crucial events or reconstructive relationships. The human being is a creative agent as well as a recipient of symbolized orders of experience.

Motivational inscriptions are hidden from reflective interpretations. This is a paradox, for needs and wishes appear closest to personal consciousness; in fact, the very inwardness of these lived interpretations makes them seem deceptively available for understanding. This apparent accessibility encouraged the existentialist concern with the symbol of the self as self-consciousness. Philosophy and theology exploited this possibility in the twentieth century. However, the very subjectivity of this pathway meant that attempts to disclose the world of the self were likely to reduce the symbolized world to personal will and decision, yet existentialism seemed the only creative alternative over against the reductionist pressures of technical and scientific autonomy. A mechanistic world of impersonal forces dwarfed the human project, reducing persons to automatons whose only meaning lay in their functions within the systems of production and consumption. Against this alienating world, existentialism asserted the self-transcending, irreducible power of self-consciousness. Radical existentialism asserted the autonomy of self-consciousness over against all structures and symbols. At this juncture, two ways opened out before the human subject: one path acknowledged the absurdity of the human project as simply the projection of the self (Camus, 1955: 1–48); the other path led in the direction of an autonomous subject who could overcome bad faith (Sartre). The existentialist claim for the self-transcending reach of the human remains a legitimate achievement which is supported by the root metaphor of artistic process. However, the creativity of the human species need not imply autonomy or independence of the symbols through which a people dwells on earth. The self dwells in and through a people, even though the self bears its own responsibility.

Psychological inquiries and therapies have disclosed this world of symbols through which the self shares the life of a people. Several prominent psychologists have explored this symbolic horizon of the self. For the most part, however, depth psychology has contented itself with attempting to decipher the dream symbolism of clients so far as it illumined inner conflicts and repressed wishes (Freud; Horney). Erik Erikson has pressed his own inquiries to the level of encompassing symbols under the rubric of ideology (Erikson, 1964). However, Carl Jung and his followers have investigated the symbolic world which binds the self as symbol to the total symbolization of a people's world (Jung). Jung likewise traced the connections between personal symbolizations and the archetypes which they disclose. This pioneering work is a testimony to the creative powers of the person which existentialism asserted; it also testifies to the symbolic mediation of the human world. Thus, the motivational structures of the self provide access to the symbolic world, yet the significance of that world is far from self-evident and calls for a disciplined hermeneutic. The interpenetration of the religious, political, familial, and other symbols in personal and public worlds can only be adequately investigated when psychological and social scientific inquiries can be shared and raised to the level of a hermeneutic of symbols. At the moment, little more than creative insights are available to guide such research, for the world of symbols has been treated as either a symptom of mental stress or as a realm of fantasy which a rational society will transcend (Fierro, 1977: chap. 8).

There is a dialogue or dialectic within the reciprocal of symbol/interpretation. There is also a dialectic in the interplay of the various modes of inscription of symbol. Cultural expressions may legitimate and inscribe institutional patterns but they may also challenge established practices or understandings. The case of Galileo is familiar, but one could as well list the innovators in the arts, philosophy, political economy, and theology. Societal praxis resists the creative visions of the innovators. However, institutional praxis has its own autonomous power, changing motivational patterns and cultural understandings through its modes of treating the world, things, and persons. The praxis of the capitalistic and socialistic systems has altered the consciousness and cultural milieu of the modern world. Both systems had their theorists but they changed the world through praxis.

The motivational mode has a certain autonomy with reference to culture and institutions, for inner transformations can alter styles of life and gradually influence the larger, societal systems. This is particularly true in the case of religious movements. Individualism in the American tradition has, to be sure, exaggerated the social significance of personal transformation, assuming that societal improvement comes about primarily through change in the attitudes of individuals. The evidence regarding change in racist attitudes and practices contradicts this naïve theory of social change, for legislative innovations have in fact altered relationships and attitudes. However, motivational transformations, especially where they take collective or communal form, can alter the social milieu in important ways. Religious and sectarian movements are sufficient evidence of such transformations to validate the importance of the motivational mode.

A dialectical interplay of symbol and lived interpretation constitutes human dwelling. This dialectic unfolds in the conflicts and reciprocities of cultural, institutional, and motivational interpretations. To say a people dwells historically means that it lives its symbolic world, sustaining those symbolic horizons in day by day activities and altering those horizons through creative interpretations. The continuity of a people's world is mediated by symbols and lived interpretations. Changes in a people's world arise through innovative interpretations; however such changes succeed when they transform the symbolic horizon. Such considerations raise a radical question about symbols, for they imply that symbols may distort and conceal human possibilities as well as disclose them.

THE SYMBOL CALLS FORTH THOUGHT

Challenges to established authority usually make appeal to the legacy of symbols, offering new interpretations or proposing an authentic interpretation. Scientists appeal to a "nature" that has not been adequately understood. Charismatic figures lay claim to the sacred heritage which has been disfigured by religious authorities. A rising bourgeois class challenges the inherited privileges of a landed aristocracy. In one way or another, traditional symbols are challenged or reinterpreted.

The symbol offers no simple court of appeal in such conflicts. The symbol is ambiguous. Dual or multiple levels of symbolic meaning present possibilities of misunderstanding. Symbols not only call forth interpretation but also demand it, for their ambiguities lead to conflicting interpretations. The folk tales, stories, and myths of traditional peoples interpret the legacy of symbols, unfolding their meanings and altering those meanings over time. Myth is an interpretative explication of symbol, even as clan organization and ritual action interpret symbolic meanings. Creation, rupture, threats of chaos and pollution, assurances of another harvest, all find appropriate interpretations in the myths and rituals of archaic peoples. Where conflicts arise, religious specialists offer a judgment and settle the case as best they can.

The ambiguity of symbol is present from the outset by virtue of the duality of literal and higher order meaning. The technological age has exploited the ambiguity of symbol, reducing higher orders of meaning to everyday interests—treating nature as energy to be amassed and manipulated, viewing sacred symbols as products of human wish and fantasy, considering the family a device for the fulfillment of individual needs for satisfaction. The duality of symbol allows for such reduction, even as metaphor always seems open to reduction by substitution; however, both modes of reduction disfigure the symbol or metaphor and obscure the horizon of meaning which the symbol mediates. Thus, symbolizations of nature, life, sacred mystery, and political life are reducible to calculable elements. The human species is left with its projects and dreams in an empty cosmos.

The ambiguity of symbol opens the way to other modes of disfigurement. If one asks why the human species exploits the ambiguity of symbol, one is probably driven to recognize the human struggle against the uncertainties of anything beyond its control. Human uncertainty is generated by the symbolic opening of the horizon of futurity, for the future is the realm of the unknown and incalculable. However, the immediate question is how the symbol lends itself to distortion. There are several ways in which this occurs.

Symbols arise in revelatory events that are ambiguous from the outset. Disclosure events obscure their own source, since the revelatory event is crystallized in a symbol that displaces its source. We see this process vividly in religious symbolizations of the sacred. Moses struggles for certainty through a sight of the source but sees only Jahweh's receding back. In asking for the name of the Holy One, he receives the ambiguous answer, "I will be who I will be." Abraham Lincoln agonizes over the decisions that confront the nation with a revolt of the Confederacy. He never receives a clear answer. Similar ambiguities attend the emergence of technology, as the myth of Prometheus suggests.

Moreover, symbolizations are limited, since they exclude even as they disclose. Kingship in Israel brought political unity but at the expense of the federated polity of the covenant of Sinai. The struggle of the prophets with the kings derived in part from the attempt to reinstate the ancient covenant. Patriarchal symbolism was paramount in the historical period of Israel, yet alternative symbolism is present in the earliest, Jahwist mythology. Patriarchal symbols triumphed and excluded other possibilities, leading to sexist distortions that are being radically questioned in our own time. In the more recent past, the American republic declared its position vis-à-vis the mother country with the words, "We, the people . . ." yet accented the individualistic aspect of human rights. In the course of capitalistic development, individual right to property displaced the people. In Robert Bellah's interpretation, the covenant of greed displaced the covenant of virtue. The partiality of symbol sets the stage for distortion in the drift of history.

Symbolic disclosures are also distorted by the strata of society which become their bearers or protagonists. This aspect of symbol fascinated Max Weber, who spoke of such strata as "affinity groups": those attracted by their position in society to the vision of a charismatic figure. Mohammed's failure to attract a significant following in Medina during the early years may well have resulted from his repudiation of the wealthy and powerful. It is evident that he changed his orientation in favor of the powerful after his move to Mecca and soon attracted worldly power with his message.[3] A prophet is perhaps without honor in the country of origin, but a prophet is powerless without an affinity group that can bear the message in the struggles of the world. Max Weber drew attention to this phenomenon in his interpretation of the role of the emerging commercial class in implementing the views of John Calvin. Rational capitalism and the emerging merchant class fitted well with an ascetic Protestantism which stressed frugality, discipline, nonmagical religion, and the conviction that worldly success was a sign of divine election to salvation. Whatever the limitations of this hypothesis on the Protestant ethic, Weber's examination of capitalism made it quite clear that the same strata who were bearers of the Protestant ethos were proponents of capitalism. Karl Marx's historical studies of Western economy drew attention to the different strata which initiated particular phases in Western economic development. In brief, symbolizations such as a market economy become historically powerful only as they are attractive to certain strata which give them concrete expression in lived interpretations.

Distortions of symbol develop as particular affinity groups become established and cling to the power which their innovative position has won. The gospel message initially attracted impoverished sectors of the Hellenistic world. By the time Christianity was established as an official religion under Constantine, the message of poverty and sacrifice was displaced to monastic communities and efforts were made to support established authority (Troeltsch, 1: 89–161). The church in the West has struggled since that time to maintain its original message without offending the powerful strata who have been its supporters. That struggle continues today in Latin America as was demonstrated in the meeting of the Catholic bishops at Puebla, Mexico, in 1979. Symbols mediate power. They can become the weapons of oppressive groups in their struggle to maintain power. Creative interpretations set the stage for lower strata of society to rise to power. In time, those strata claim "possession" of the symbols which empowered them. At this stage, only revolutionary praxis can liberate the symbols from their guardians.

An obvious solution to the ambiguity of symbols would be to dispose of symbolization and confine our "world" to rational instruments of manipulation and control. This was the dream of the Enlightenment and continues to be the project of positivistic thought. Such projects attempt to reduce the world to manageable entities. They succeed only insofar as they suppress the symbolic horizons which shape their consciousness and actions; thus, they become ideological distortions of their own commitments, posing as objective while disposing of the world on their own terms. People dwell symbolically and only so do they dwell historically. To deny historicality in the name of objective rationality is only to suppress the source of power and truth through which any people can dwell in justice and peace. The stratum that claims an absolute truth has simply taken possession of the symbolization of truth in order to establish its own authority. There is no immediate, prelinguistic, presymbolic access to reality which would lend final authority to any religious, political, scientific, or other bastion of power. Symbolic disclosures gain historical power through the lived interpretations of particular strata; in turn, those disclosures become the distorted instruments of legitimation of oppression by the same strata.

The dialectic of symbolic distortion and lived interpretation sheds light on the ambiguous term *ideology* which emerged with the sociological tradition. The Marxist tradition gave prominence to the notion of ideology, designating by the term a false consciousness that serves to conceal the economic interests of those in power by legitimating their position (Marx, 1938). Karl Mannheim developed this line of thought about ideology, contrasting it with utopian thought which projected a class-based interest in revolutionary transformation of the society (Mannheim, 1936). Thus, ideology represented at once the legitimation of repressive forces and the utopian projection of a new society.

Clifford Geertz attempted to rehabilitate this positive notion of ideology, proposing that ideologies are metaphoric projections of alternative futures. He argued for the necessity of such "models for" reality (ideologies) in political processes in contrast to scientific "models of" reality (Geertz: chap. 8).

The term *ideology* has oscillated between the two poles of false consciousness and projection of a viable future in much of the recent literature (Gouldner: chaps. 1 and 2). The term *ideology* is so ambiguous that Juan Luis Segundo employs it in the sense both of false consciousness and of projection of a workable future (Segundo: chaps. 1 and 4). One could argue that Segundo was simply being careless in his use of terms, but knowing the clarity of his work one is inclined to assume that ideology can mean both distortion of and "model for." The question is how the term can be useful if it carries this double meaning.

The dialectic of symbol/interpretation in historical dwelling clarifies some of the confusion that attends the term *ideology*. Ideologies are the myths of the politico-economic world. They are the hermeneutic of political and economic symbols. If we take as an example the ideology of "Blaming the Victim" which has been so prominent in America, this understanding of ideology as politico-economic myth sheds considerable light on its validity and distortion (Ryan: chap. 1). William Ryan has shown that American people, by which he means primarily the middle class, view those who are poor, black, marginalized, or excluded from the socioeconomic advantages of the affluent society as blamable for their condition. Whatever the particular pathology, poverty, ill health, poor housing, lack of employment, it is charged to the victims. This may be done in one of two ways. In the traditional wisdom, the poor may simply be indicted as genetically inferior. More recent ideological formulations attribute the failure of the poor to earlier conditioning through the slave culture or deprivation or some version of the vicious circle of poverty. In any case, the outcome of the analysis seems logical. The fault exists within the circumstances of the victims of poverty, not within the social system which oppresses them. Consequently, the social system escapes serious criticism while the victims are made the cause of their own difficulties.

The remarkable fact about the ideology of blaming the victim is that it seems resistant to critical, rational refutation and is sometimes shared by the victims upon whom it is imposed. The striking paradox of this ideology is that it is fostered by social scientists and spread through the society in popular and academic publications (Gordon: introduction and chap. 5). How can such a false understanding remain so influential in the light of contradictory evidence? How can such false consciousness be classified under the term *ideology* when ideology can also mean a "model for" liberating action?

Political process seems to require a mythology of politico-economic symbols. This is the truth in Clifford Geertz's insight and Segundo's investigation of religious and political ideologies. Segundo is arguing that religious faith is a way of life and, therefore, involves a projection of a future that is inescapably political. Thus, religious life involves explicitly or implicitly a political ideology. Drawing again on the idea of affinity groups who are bearers of a particular, historical symbolization, it is evident that positive ideologies are the projections by such groups of a meaningful religio-political future. In this sense, Israel's covenant or the American republic were ideological projections of liberating futures that were borne by particular groups who aspired to power or leadership (Gottwald). The implicit limitations and ambiguities of such ideologies can become distorted in time, yet bearers of the ideology cling to their power, reasserting the ideology against the historical actualities. The balance shifts away from projection of a liberating future toward false consciousness. The ideology becomes, in fact, a mask of the real conditions of the people and their authentic future. However, the ideology draws its power from the symbolic foundations of the people's life which it claims to interpret. The kings in Israel invoked the religious authority of the covenant of kingship while their actions disfigured the responsibility of the king to Jahweh and the people. Similarly, the ideology of blaming the victim draws on the symbolization of the free market; as long as the failure of twenty to thirty percent of the population to make a place for themselves in the market can be blamed on their own defects, the market economy can be protected from challenge. Since the market economy is proving less and less viable in the conditions of global, corporate capitalism and administered markets in oil, food, etc., market symbolization no longer projects a liberating future for the mass of people. The political mythology thus becomes a distortion of reality, legitimating the power of an affinity group who no longer bear a creative future. In the case of Israel, the distortions of kingship led finally to disaster. In the case of blaming the victim, the distortions of socio-economic life pave the way for major economic dislocations. Ideologies function in these circumstances to conceal the truth about conditions.

The significance of this reinterpretation of the ambiguous term *ideology* is that it shifts attention away from the subjective interests of one or another group to the symbolization that constitutes the world of a people and the role of particular groups as interpreters of the symbols. So long as ideology was reduced to collective interests, all political thought was reducible to ideology. One could argue that only one's opponents were ideologists. When ideology is understood as interpretation of symbol (political mythology), then approporiate or inappropriate, false or liberating ideological proposals can be evaluated in terms of a people's struggle for justice. Masking or enlightening ideologies can then be judged in terms of the liberating future which they project. Where that future violates justice and the public happiness, ideology eclipses the horizon of hope which the symbol mediates. Where a liberating future opens, ideology orients dwelling to the promise of the symbol.

Although several terms have been used to indicate a liberating ideological projection, these terms fail to determine clearly which ideology is appropriate in a people's history. Every group or nation claims that its ideology is the one that will yield a promising future. There is no avoiding the question of adequate grounds for a critique of ideology and for determining appropriate ideological projections. If one accepts with Juan Luis Segundo the notion that every project in life, including that of faith, involves ideological projection, then the question remains as to how one evaluates the historical struggle for justice and peace. What makes one ideology liberating and another degrading?

Archetypal directionalities furnish criteria of fulfillment or distortion in a people's dwelling. Only the actual histories of various peoples provide direct access to such directionalities. However, rather discernible norms of justice order human relationships, work, engagements with nature, political order, and personal development. Because of modern preoccupation with the symbol of the self, we have learned much more about "developmentals" or basic directionalities of personal maturation than about the directionalities of economic or political life. The work of Erik Erikson and others has clarified certain directions in personality development which may be altered but not eradicated by particular cultural heritages (Yankelovich and Barrett: 386–404). This is an important clue to archetypal directionalities. They are universal but disclosed only through the symbols and lived interpretations of particular peoples. The very possibility of understanding peoples of different symbolic traditions rests upon this universal infrastructure which finds expression in a common humanity.

The symbolic heritage and its various interpretations provide guideposts to the experience of a people and crossculturally to human experience through the ages. We are not left without testimony to the evil forces of injustice, exploitation, tyranny, and holocaust. Religious and political traditions, whatever their distortions, furnish guideposts in the struggle of peoples to find their way to a more just, peaceful, and sustainable life. In this framework, we can discern the illusion of the Enlightenment that a people can dispense with tradition and reduce its world to rational projects (Davis: chaps. 4 and 6). So far as the Enlightenment confirms human responsibility in the appropriation of its heritage, it is a crucial defense against distortion. So far as it asserts that tradition is arbitrary authority, it confuses the authority of tradition with a heteronomous power. The legacy of symbols is authoritative only insofar as it crystallizes ways that foster justice, truth, goodness, and peace.

In the final analysis, the experience of peoples, their well-being or suffering, the fulfillment of their aspirations to freedom and justice, or the disappointment of their dreams, furnish crucial insight into archetypal directionalities and moral imperatives.

The human species is finally responsible for discernment of the quality of its life and the justice or injustice of its relationships. This brings us back to our earlier consideration of who is to be the bearer of a liberating future. If an appropriate ideology is one borne by an affinity group representing the people's hope for justice, then it is within this context that a critique of ideologies must occur. Critical reflection on a people's future would thus have to take place in the context of the struggle for a just and peaceful future among those who are bearers of that future. Latin American theologians have stressed this matter of social context of theological and political reflection. They locate their hermeneutic work amidst the poor, following in this respect the prophetic tradition of locating the divine word among the poor and oppressed. This hermeneutic privilege of the oppressed establishes the context of critique if one is ready to claim with the prophets that the word of the Lord, the constitutive power of the future of a people, takes its stand with the poor. James Cone has made a similar claim for the privilege of black people in the American experience (Cone). Liberation theology challenges political and social interpretation as well as theological hermeneutics, for it raises questions about any reflective interpretation which identifies itself with the established authorities who have the most to gain by perpetuating distorting ideologies.

These general remarks on interpretation lead us to the question of how one reads the societal text within an artistic paradigm. If we can specify the method for such a task, it should be possible to explore the horizon of religious and moral possibilities that would constitute a liberating future for our time.

READING THE SOCIETAL TEXT

Reading a text, according to Ricoeur's theory of interpretation, involves both understanding and explanation. Understanding has traditionally been associated with cultural inquiries such as history. Explanation has been associated with the inquiries of the exact sciences, aiming at the formulation of causal laws or uniformities. These two approaches have been rather sharply distinguished, although major figures such as Wilhelm Dilthey and Max Weber attempted to work out a synthesis of understanding and explanation. Dilthey sought a method of understanding which could achieve exactitude by understanding the intention of the author of the cultural work. The comprehension of the author's intention would be understanding the "cause" of the work. Max Weber attempted to synthesize understanding and explanation by a theory of causal adequacy, presuming that an explanation would be valid if the expected sequence fitted our understanding of how things worked in society. Weber was conscious of the fact that understanding was the guiding force in his work, however, since the causal sequence was an attempt to trace what had already been grasped by a sense of adequacy of meaning (Weber, 1949: pt. III). Paul Ricoeur has attempted a reconciliation of these methods in reading a text. He has also treated the analogy of the text to action and the writing of history, thus confirming the present project of seeing the work of art (text) as analogue to lived interpretations in human dwelling (action) (Ricoeur, 1978: chap. 11).

Three moments or steps are interwoven in Ricoeur's proposal for a method of reading a text: (1) guessing or discerning the character of the text as a whole; (2) analytical explanation of the structure of the text such that the immanent sense of the text emerges; (3) comprehension of the referential meaning of the text, the world that it projects (Ricoeur, 1976: chap. 4). The first and third moments are nonmethodic in that they involve an understanding grasp of the text and a being grasped by or appropriated to the world projected by the text. The second moment is methodic in the sense of tracing a causal sequence in the interrelation of the parts. In Ricoeur's way of speaking of texts, moments one and three are semantic illuminations of the meaning of the text, and moment two is a semiotic of the grammatical structure of the text. His aim in taking this approach to the text is to show how a semiotic of the text presupposes a semantic of the text (the guess) and eventuates in a semantic appropriation (comprehension); by the same token, he is attempting to show how a semantic of the text involves and even requires a semiotic of the structure of the text in order to clarify the guess. Taking some liberty with Ricoeur's method, I shall follow the moments of reading of the text, extending the analogue of the text to a reflective interpretation of human dwelling.

1. Guessing or Discerning

The preliminary construing of the text concerns the work as a whole. It is decisive whether the text be read as a poem, historical document, myth, or parable. This sense of the whole is something like a gestalt, a discerning of the character of the whole with which one is dealing. Guesses, as Ricoeur notes, are not simply arbitrary leaps but can be validated, or at least tested, by various modes of converging indices. Some guesses are better than others and a case can be made for the preference of one choice over others. The importance of this first moment in the reading of the text is that it locates the text by genre, descrying the kind of coding that generates the text as a whole, hence, indicating the analytic tools that will be appropriate for exploring the deeper structure of the text. Furthermore, the guess indicates the horizon of sense which is relevant in exploring the text. In brief, the guess is prescriptive as well as descriptive, since it establishes systems of relevances even as it identifies the totality to be explored.

In a reflective interpretation of human dwelling the guess may function on various levels. The preceding chapters have unfolded a guess on the macro-level of human dwelling, arguing that an artistic process is our best clue to understanding human life and history. Root metaphors are, in this sense, guesses or discerning intuitions of the character of the totality of life and cosmos. Such encompassing guesses furnish clues to the symbolized world enacted in lived interpretations. From day to day people treat things, other persons, and the meanings that guide their actions according to some such clue as to how things fit together and which things take priority. In reflective interpretations, guesses may also function as paradigms or social theories, guiding inquiries and selecting particular kinds of data as appropriate. Ideologies, in this sense, unfold societal or political guesses in myths.

Various perspectives on racism in the United States exemplify the importance of the guess in guiding thought and action.

Racism is a radically distorted symbolization of what it means to be human, a distortion that persists stubbornly in American consciousness and institutions. Racism is viewed by some thoughtful people as a matter of personal taste; thus, Milton Friedman proposed that some people like those of different color and others do not (Friedman). Racism has also been attributed to inherent defects of certain groups of people which warrant treating them as lesser beings. This is the implication of Edward Banfield's interpretation of the character of poor people in the ghettoes (Banfield). Daniel Moynihan attributed the difficulties of black people to defects in their family life, assuming that the black family was inadequate for urban life (Moynihan). Racism has also been attributed to the economic forces of capitalism which perpetuate a cheap pool of labor. Gunnar Myrdal, on the other hand, attributed the intractable force of racism to a lack of moral determination on the part of the American people to live up to their ideals of freedom and equal opportunity (Myrdal). More recently George Pickering proposed that the "color line" is a religious structure shaping the understanding of reality and priority of values in American life (Pickering). This last proposal opens the symbolism of racism to reflection, going beyond description of institutional forces in which the distorted symbolization is inscribed.

Paul Ricoeur argues that guesses are not arbitrary but can be tested for their cogency. The same holds for reading the societal text, and in this instance opening an inquiry into racism in America. Such guesses finally have to be tested against structures of dwelling in order to assess their plausibility. This is always a somewhat circular process since the guess shapes the relevant data and the kinds of answers that are entertained as fitting. Attributing racism to a matter of taste, for example, simply fails to account for the systemic patterning of racism in particular sectors of the society. Blaming the victim by attributing racism to defects of particular peoples or their family life also fails to deal with data, for similar people of like background, under conditions where work and income are available, prove to be productive and healthy. The guess is a "tacit knowledge" that opens the way to tracing the sequences that generate a particular phenomenon. Some guesses support ideologies that conceal social realities.

2. Explanation

Explanation traces the deep structure of the text. It is analytic, breaking the whole into its parts and tracing out the dynamic process that generates the whole. Ricoeur uses the structuralist approach to the text as paradigmatic for this moment. He follows Lévi-Strauss's work on myth which treats the mythic text as deriving its sense strictly from grammatical coding. Because this is a universal coding for Lévi-Strauss, all myths and works of human dwelling follow the same basic structure of mind and eventuate in the resolution of the same basic contradictions. Paul Ricoeur is primarily concerned to show how such an explanatory method presupposes a guess as to the existential contradictions worked out in cultural creations. In brief, Ricoeur denies that explanation is an autonomous process which can unfold the meanings of culture without presuppositions. In Ricoeur's perspective, methodic explanation of the infrastructure of the text presupposes understanding (the guess) and traces the appropriate coding. He also repudiates the attempt of the structuralists to settle for the immanent sense of the text, prescinding from the referential meaning which the text projects. He notes, for example, that Lévi-Strauss understands myth as "making men aware of certain oppositions and of tending toward their progressive mediation" (Ricoeur, 1976: 87). To this extent, the structuralist approach presupposes a world of oppositions and mediations while refusing to subject this projected world to reflection. It reduces the text to its immanent sense. Explanation, thus, opens inevitably for Ricoeur on comprehension of the world projected in the text, even though prejudices of certain explanatory approaches may suppress this level of understanding.

Social scientific interpretations of human dwelling have tended to settle for explanatory methods. In *Elements for a Social Ethic* the present author attempted to sort out various styles and indicate the appropriateness of different styles of human science for particular tasks (Winter, 1966: chap. 6). In a root metaphor approach to lived interpretation, these styles of social science can be identified with mechanistic, organicist, and artistic images. The physicalist or behaviorist style develops its explanatory procedures from a mechanistic understanding of life and cosmos. The functionalist and voluntarist styles are variants of organicism, the former considering the functioning of parts within the whole and the voluntarist attending to the motivational aspect of the lived interpretations within an organic whole. The intentionalist style was projected as an option for disclosing the higher order meanings that inform human dwelling. That proposal can now be clarified. It pointed toward a style of human science that would take seriously the world projected in the lived interpretations of dwelling. In brief, the intentionalist style insists on carrying the task of understanding beyond the immanent sense of dwelling to its referential meanings, or what Ricoeur calls the moment of comprehension.

Interpreting racism highlights the importance of extending reflective interpretation to the level of comprehension. Most explanatory approaches reduce phenomena to certain causal sequences and the immanent sense that their own methods impose. Edward Banfield, following a mechanistic approach to the urban situation, assumed a free play of entities in a market. Since certain entities did not fit his model of the market and since he was unwilling to question the appropriateness of the model, his only option was to attribute friction in the mechanism to defects in certain of the entities. Those entities in his model happened to be primarily black and minority peoples. Talcott Parsons's structural functionalism employs an organicist model. The system is taken as a whole and various parts are treated as functional or dysfunctional, much like the organs in the human body. Since black people were not functioning in the system and since the system is presumed to be adequate, the problem must be *in* the black people who need to be made more adaptive to the system (Parsons and Clark). The obvious answer is to upgrade blacks and minority people who seem to be excluded from the system. The problem of racism is thus projected onto the victims who do not fit into the system. Restricting thought to the immanent sense of the societal text means that the guess and the method of reading the text are not really open to challenge, for the method confirms the guess and the guess undergirds the method. In terms of Gadamer's hermeneutical theory, the preunderstanding which always guides interpretation is controlled by method rather than by the disclosure power of the text. Since these inquiries were being implemented in public policies, they took the form of self-fulfilling prophecies which reinforced their unreflected findings.

An artistic metaphor affirms yet transcends the immanent sense of societal process, since a work of art projects a world within the work itself through the quality of the experience it generates. A work of art mediates a quality of experience that corresponds to its immanent sense. One can always let the matter rest there, enjoying the experience and appreciating the work. However, as John Dewey observed, the artistic process generates a moral and spiritual vision that enhances and enriches the everyday world beyond its prosaic limits (Dewey: 195). The immanent sense is not self-contained. The methods that trace the immanent sense are lived interpretations in the cultural mode, projecting a world by their very structure. They can only be tested as their findings are seen within the symbolic horizon they project. The adequacy of interpretation of symbol can only be tested by the symbol of justice in a people's legacy of symbols. Guesses and methods that fail this test require careful reconsideration. George Pickering has raised this issue in his essay "The Color Line." He presses reflection to the larger vision of human reality that is inscribed in racist interpretations. In the context of our inquiry, this referential sense is precisely the symbolic horizon that founds and sometimes distorts our world. Lived interpretations, racist and other, are not self-contained, causal sequences but inscriptions of a symbolized world of life and cosmos in everyday dwelling. Proposals by Milton Friedman, Gary Becker, Edward Banfield, Kenneth Clark, and others can only be tested against the symbolization of a just society and the struggle for justice by black America. This is finally a religious and moral question. Perspectives on human dwelling ultimately involve an understanding of the human world, of justice and of the things that make for peace and community. These are religio-moral questions that are mediated by the legacy of symbols.

3. Comprehension

In Ricoeur's theory of the text, comprehension is an event of appropriation of the reader to the world projected in the text. He speaks of narrative, for example, as redescribing the world, luring us into that reality, illumining our possibilities. Appropriation to the referential sense of the text is not taking possession of the text. It is rather being transformed by the disclosure power of the text—being appropriated to the world of the text.

In appropriation to the text (comprehension), one is enabled to participate in the world opened by the text. Ricoeur gives an existentialist interpretation of this event of appropriation, following the path of much of his earlier work:

> Only the interpretation that complies with the injunction of the text, that follows the "arrow" of the sense and that tries to think accordingly, initiates a new self-understanding. In this self-understanding, I would oppose the self, which proceeds from the understanding of the text, to the ego, which claims to precede it. It is the text, with its universal power of world disclosure, which gives a self to the ego. [Ricoeur, 1976: 95]

Ricoeur's focus on the self and self-understanding reveals an implicit sense of comprehension which he does not discuss. Comprehension is essentially the opening of the symbolized world by the text, empowering participation in this world. In the framework of the foregoing reflections, the text empowers participation in the symbols that shape and order our world. Paul Ricoeur's existentialist preunderstanding raises the symbolization of the self to the position of priority. However, the self may not be the most important symbolization that comes to disclosure in the text. I shall argue in chapter 4 that creation is the paramount symbolization that is being disclosed in our time and that the self can best be resymbolized in the context of that creative process. For the moment, the issue is the significance of the moment of comprehension in the reading of the text. In this regard, one should bear in mind Ricoeur's stress, in the passage cited above, upon following the "'arrow' of the sense" of the text. The symbolizations of world opened in the text are not extraneous to the text, as though the text were to be read as "having a message." The immanent sense of the text, the quality of the experience it mediates, is itself mediation of that symbolic world. This is important for the interpretation of human dwelling in our own time, because the symbolic world has been eclipsed by our attention to pragmatic processes of managing, coping, and controlling. In this sense, the reductionism of human science is merely a reflection of a reductionistic loss of sense of the totality in the lived interpretations of our technologized society. When one explores the religious or ultimate horizons of our contemporary world, one finds them inscribed in the immanent sense of everyday, lived interpretations—motivational systems, cultural expressions, institutionalized praxis, racism, and struggles for justice. The humanities and the sciences do not operate in self-contained universes. They are modes of lived interpretation of a symbolized world. The all-consuming devotion to accumulation of wealth in our time does not reflect an ineradicable human nature. This is a motivational inscription of a symbolization of the world that distorts the human and its place in the cosmos. Comprehension is an event arising from the contradictions within the immanent sense of lived interpretations and their distortions. This is the dialectic where faith and unfaith, truth and untruth, justice and injustice are encountered and decided.

This interpretation recasts Ricoeur's discussion of comprehension of the text in terms of participation in the symbolization that the text discloses. Appropriation to the world projected in the text is, in this sense, appropriation to the symbolized world of meaning that a lived interpretation mediates. One can similarly recast George Pickering's work on the "color line." Color is a medium of symbolization that has distorted the American sense of what it means to be human. Whatever the roots of this distorted symbolization, it can only be transformed by critical cultural expressions and a different praxis. Overcoming segregated living arrangements and schooling have altered distorted symbolization of race, opening the way to different motivations and practices. Unless one raises reflections on dwelling to the level of symbol, the empowering and distorting role of symbolization is concealed. Transformation of distorted symbolization does not occur through a direct challenge to symbols. Pietistic thinking in America assumes it is possible to alter racism by achieving a proper faith or inward orientation. Such a faith perspective may be helpful but only as it is articulated in different institutional arrangements and cultural interpretations. The vision of a human world of freedom and equality only transforms dwelling as it is inscribed in social, economic, political, and religious institutions.

America has yet to deal seriously with the religious distortion inscribed in its racism. Lillian Smith traced this distortion in a telling way in her fine work, *Killers of the Dream.* The reading of the societal text has to penetrate both lived interpretations and symbolic horizons if renewal and transformation are to issue from such reflection. Reflective interpretation does not alter our disfigured world, but it can contribute to the practical tasks of creative, lived interpretations that implement an authentic religio-moral praxis.

THE RELIGIO-MORAL HORIZON

Paul Ricoeur's theory of the text has been modified to allow for understanding the referential sense of the text as disclosure of symbol. The text empowers participation in symbol. Every text, at least implicitly, opens out upon the symbolized world. This assertion has important implications for interpretations of human dwelling. It indicates that a value-neutral or merely "objective" reading of the text of human dwelling is impossible. One cannot plunge into the pains and struggles of personal life and societal dislocation without commitment for or against those struggles. To be objective is not to be neutral but to be open to conflicting interpretations. The moral and ultimate meanings of these struggles are lived out in the interpretations of people's lives, so distinctions of moral from religious discourse or scientific from moral interpretation are provisional abstractions which finally cohere in the symbols. Refusal to deal with this level of comprehension, except as a provisional bracketing of issues for a particular purpose, is ideological concealment since it masks commitments and imperatives.

The religio-moral character of dwelling poses questions of true and false readings, right and wrong interpretations, moral and immoral patterns of relationship. Reflective interpretation cannot escape these questions any more than lived interpretation can avoid the moral and ultimate commitments which confront people day by day. Yet there is no absolute determination of the true and false, distorted and authentic symbolizations. Peoples dwell historically within a symbolized world, testing interpretations in experience, testing the words of the true and false prophets against the legacy of symbols. The moral imperatives of dwelling issue from symbolic disclosures of right, justice, good faith, and peace. They come to light in the inner dialectic between the promise of symbols such as justice and the distortion of such symbols in lived interpretations such as racism, sexism, or imperialism. The religious possibilities of dwelling issue from the promise of completion that is mediated in symbols such as creation and redemption, liberty and commonwealth. But the particular actions and institutional arrangements which express those imperatives and hopes cannot be settled by fiat or authority. Such policy imperatives are settled by reflection, persuasion, and commitments in life.

Nevertheless, moral and religious claims can be discussed in reasonable fashion. Here the discerning guess or metaphoric network is of the first importance. The artistic process offers important clues to the moral and religious aspects of human dwelling. In speaking of symbols as events in an artistic process, one is opening a horizon of understanding of the meaning of religion and morality for this age. If this religio-moral understanding can be clarified, it should be possible to illumine the meaning of the sacred in this techno-scientific age.

NOTES

1. The term *praxis* is current among liberation theologians. They are attempting to overcome the separation of thought and action in theology and the social sciences. Praxis is treated here as the lived interpretations that achieve structural form in socio-political and economic institutions. For a helpful analysis of the status of praxis in

current theology, see Matthew Lamb's "The Theory-Praxis Relationship in Contemporary Christian Theologies" (Lamb).

2. This interpretation of temporality is drawn from Martin Heidegger's hermeneutic in *Being and Time* (Heidegger, 1962: div. 2, chaps. 4–6). The translation of *Dasein* as symbol has been prepared by the interpretation of the self in chap. 2. It also has some warrant in Heidegger's later work.

3. The author is indebted to Anwar Barkat for this interpretation, presented in a lecture at Princeton Theological Seminary, Spring, 1980.

4

THE LIBERATION OF CREATION

M. M. Thomas, the ecumenical theologian and ethicist from South India, made a telling comment after a semester of teaching in the United States.[1] He observed that the students evinced little or no sense of the spirituality of corporate life. By the same token, he felt that the life of the particular seminary in question, the curriculum, and the general atmosphere of American society contributed to this spiritual impoverishment. By "spirituality of corporate life," Dr. Thomas meant the religious and moral qualities that inhere in or are excluded from social, economic, and political institutions. He was drawing attention to the privatization of religious sensibility in American life. He was also implying that the restriction of spirituality to personal inwardness impoverished corporate life, eroding the sense of justice.

Social critics have also drawn attention to this lack of corporate concern in American life. Richard Sennett speaks of a narcissistic age (Sennett). Christopher Lasch employs the image of narcissism to depict the alienation of the modern age (Lasch). Such psychological images may exaggerate societal conditions but they illumine trends and moods. Narcissism suggests a turning toward the self, viewing the surrounding world only in its enhancement of or threat to the self (Kohut). A friend, for example, only remains a friend so long as he or she enhances one's own self-importance. Narcissism is a pathological preoccupation with one's own sense of worth. It is a radical image of egocentricity which certainly has to be employed with caution. However, it does reflect the breakdown in public involvements and communal concerns in recent decades. Whether this eclipse of the public arises from narcissistic turning toward the self or from the breakdown of communal networks is a matter for inquiry. Nevertheless, the image of narcissism identifies a societal condition that threatens citizenship and public responsibility.

The erosion of communal concerns is almost taken for granted in American life. A personal style of life is the preoccupying value for most people. Style of life is cultivated by advertising and exploited by industry. Communal solidarity and responsibility are seldom even mentioned among the values of this consumer society. Religious and moral qualities are viewed primarily as personal or private matters. Even the Moral Majority, which played such a significant part in the 1980 electoral campaign in the United States, focused on issues of private morality. There was no discussion of the injustices of escalating unemployment and poverty in urban and rural areas. Even the judgments imposed on the public sector in the 1980 campaign represented a regimen of private morality. The issue of the Panama Canal was raised, but only as a test of personal patriotism. Public symbols of human rights, self-determination of other peoples, and hopes for peace versus nuclear holocaust were eclipsed or repressed. The relevant symbols of sacred reality are those of individual morality and the inwardness of personal life. However important such symbols may be, they mediate a truncated religious and moral world. Erosion of public life ultimately entails the loss of an authentically private sphere. This is the irony of the Moral Majority's program, for they strive to impose public restrictions on personal behavior in the name of individual freedom and free enterprise. The eclipse of the symbols of corporate responsibility prepares the way for manipulation of those symbols by special interest groups. Public symbols do not disappear. They are repressed to unconscious levels of experience, making them vulnerable to manipulation by demagogues. The Nazi movement was just such a manipulative force, raised to the level of a demonic, historical power.

Global economic dislocations are preparing the ground for more such destructive movements. However, there is also a profound hunger for justice and peace in the world. But these constructive forces lack control of the media. They do not hold the instruments of production. Nevertheless, they could be bearers of the spiritual power of corporate symbols. By contrast, the destructive forces distort symbols of national identity and religious faith. They tap the latent power of popular hunger for security and peace. Thus, future peace depends upon a liberation of religious and moral symbols from distortion. Liberation involves criticism of symbolic distortions and discovery of appropriate interpretations of the religio-moral foundations of a new age.

Such considerations require concrete, historical proposals. One such highly exemplary proposal can be examined and evaluated in the struggle over land rights in the Northwest of Canada.[2] The Mackenzie Valley Pipeline Inquiry disclosed the contesting forces in this struggle when a pipeline and energy corridor were proposed for this river valley (Berger: 1977). Forces of the techno-age and traditional human communities were confronting one another in northern Canada, reflecting similar struggles going on throughout the third world and in the central cities of urban areas. Basically this confrontation is over competing ideologies, symbol systems, and life commitments. Because this particular example of such confrontation is so applicable to other larger conflicts, I want to examine it in some detail.

THE CRISIS OF WESTERN SPIRITUALITY

The issue of a pipeline and energy corridor in the Mackenzie River Valley of northern Canada emerged with the discovery of gas in Prudhoe Bay in 1968. In the next years, Arctic Gas and other oil and gas interests in Canada and the United States worked on a proposal to transport gas from the bay across nothern Alaska and the Yukon into the Mackenzie Delta and down the river valley to southern Canada and the United States. This was to be the largest capital project engaged in by private enterprise up to that time. It had the support of the Canadian government. However, it was evident that social, economic, and environmental effects would have to be considered. The government appointed the Honorable Mr. Justice Thomas R. Berger to conduct an inquiry into the social and environmental impact of the proposed pipeline (Gamble). The Mackenzie Valley Pipeline Inquiry soon uncovered a basic conflict of interests between corporate (indirectly transnational) capitalism and native peoples of the North. This conflict raised issues of environmental damage, problems of cultural sovereignty, and ultimately questions about the future of Canada.

The story of the inquiry has been told in various forms, not to mention the eminently readable reports by the commission of inquiry (Berger, 1977). However, as I have said, certain aspects of the inquiry shed light on the spiritual crisis that has been generated by the mechanistic age, aspects which merit careful consideration. The power of corporate capitalism which drives the technological machine is manifest in the allocation of funds to preparatory studies for the pipeline. The Berger inquiry finally spent about 5.3 million dollars. It funded independent interest groups such as the Indian Brotherhood of the Northwest and the Northern Assessment Group of environmentalists. It also conducted informal hearings in the communities throughout the North in addition to the formal hearings in the South. This staggering task was executed in a year and a half and will probably remain unique, not to say historic, among such inquiries. Nevertheless, this enormous outlay of funds and expenditure of human energies could not compare with the roughly 50 million dollars expended by the corporate gas interests in preparatory studies (Berger, 1980). The imbalance in the funding of such studies reflects the David and Goliath character of the struggle that takes place throughout the world between global economic interests and local or national communities.

Early in the inquiry representatives of environmental interests challenged the adequacy of the data gathered by the corporate interests. Data or facts are inevitably selected and interpreted;

hence, other groups with different interests would also have to set up studies of social and environmental impact. It also became evident that scientific and technical experts were not the only sources of significant information on the environment and future of the North (Hutchinson and Winter). Local people from northern communities, the Dene, Inuit, Metis, and whites, were able to shed considerable light on the problems which an energy corridor would create for the environment and local people. This was, of course, even more true with respect to the future of native communities, economic development, and aspirations for political self-determination. The title of the report, *Northern Frontier, Northern Homeland,* sums up the struggle between local peoples and the politico-economic interests of technologized capitalism. The Canadian lands to the west, much like the West of the United States, had been exploited as a frontier for settlement and development. Such native peoples as survived this territorial expansion were reduced to dependency and their communities practically destroyed. Northern expansion meant a repetition of this destructive process and also threatened a fragile environment which might not survive such violent intrusions. The tragedy of western expansion was now to be magnified by the annihilation of communities and environments of the North. A fundamental question facing the inquiry was whether the peoples of the North were expendable and on what religio-moral foundations such a decision could be made.

In its final report, the commission recommended that a moratorium of ten years be imposed, allowing time for the settlement of land claims, development of native self-determination, and establishment of environmental safeguards. The inquiry was, in fact, supporting native claims. It affirmed their local economy of renewable resources against excessive dependence on a wage economy. Modern techniques had been appropriated by native people for hunting, trapping, fishing, and gathering in the northern communities; however, the economy of renewable resources furnished roughly forty percent of subsistence and cash income (Watkins: 21–85). It became apparent that native peoples participated in the wage economy largely in order to finance the tools for their bush economy. The intrusion of economic and governmental agencies from the South had, to be sure, undermined much of the local community life. The pathologies of marginalized communities—alcoholism, crime, welfare dependency, family disintegration, and erosion of communal life—had long since begun to undermine communal life. The resurgence of communal vitality in the Indian Brotherhood and other community movements indicated that native peoples were at a crossroads, extinction or new life. The inquiry supported their final bid for survival. It recognized the interdependence of the native economy of renewable resources and the hope for preservation of the wildlife and vegetation of the fragile northern environment. Although the inquiry anticipated that in time an energy corridor could be constructed, allowing for the preservation of certain areas and safeguards for the peoples and environment, it definitely sided with native peoples in their aspiration for self-determination.

There is a significant clue to the spiritual grounds of the pipeline controversy in an ideological conflict which surfaced in the wake of the report. The inquiry had become personally identified with Justice Thomas H. Berger, the commissioner. The conclusions of the report represented his ideological formulation of a possible future for native peoples in the context of Canadian development. Ideology, as was indicated in the preceding chapter, faces in two directions. It is a Januslike phenomenon. Ideology may be primarily oriented to preserving and legitimating the established powers in a society. It may also face primarily toward the future and project a utopian model for a more just society. In either case, ideology draws upon the symbolic powers that generate a people's identity, whether to legitimate powers that be or to authorize proposals for transformation. The report of the inquiry projected a model for the future that struck a balance between preserving the land claims and aboriginal rights of the native peoples while recognizing the legitimate interests of the people of the South in gaining access to resources deemed necessary for a consumer society.

The clash between Arctic Gas, representing corporate capitalism, and the native peoples is a conflict between radically different interpretations of human life, community, and nature.

The ideological projections, in brief, reflect fundamentally different paradigms or root metaphors of the world. Technological development, as we noted in chapter 1, unfolds a mechanistic paradigm of linear forces, calculating rationality, and manipulative control. Native peoples continue to dwell within an organicist world of interdependence, communal participation, and commitment to the sacredness of the world. This sense of the sacral interrelatedness of life was poignantly expressed by a group of Yukon Indians as follows:

> For many years before we heard about the white man, our people, who lived in what is now called the Yukon, lived in a different way. We lived in small groups and moved from one place to another at different times of the year. . . . Sometimes we gathered together in larger groups to fish and relax after a hard winter.
>
> We had our own God and our own religion that taught us to live in peace together. This religion also taught us how to live as part of the land. We learned how to practice what you people call multiple land use and conservation and resource management. We have something to teach white men if they will listen to us. [McCullum: 78f.]

It would be a mistake to romanticize the situation of native peoples of the North or the struggles of their past. They realize better than anyone, as can be gathered from the hearings, that their traditional ways are precariously balanced against the intrusive forces of technological development. They also realize that they will have to alter their patterns of communal life and economic organization in the future. However, they claim the right to make these adjustments in their own ways and by their own decisions. This is the historical, self-determining quality which has emerged within the organicist heritages of various peoples throughout the third world. The clash between mechanistic and organicist paradigms is not a clash of traditional and modern rational societies as is often presumed in treatments of modernization (Geertz: chap. 9). The conflict is rather between root metaphors or paradigms of historical development. Both paradigms generate a sense of history and awareness of the capacity of peoples to shape the future.

The mechanistic paradigm projects development as the expansion of human powers of control and exploitation. The virtues of this paradigm are all too evident. It has cultivated analytic science and large-scale, technological organization. These scientific forces have also played an important part in challenging dogmatic authorities in politics and religion, liberating human capacities from traditional authorities. The organicist paradigm of historical development, by contrast, locates real power in the integrity of peoples and communities, thus giving priority to sharing in the goods and sufferings of the community, cultivating bonds among peoples, nature, and the sacred. There are, of course, many variations in organicist ideologies. The hallmarks of the modern age are a sense of historical change and a recognition of a plurality of peoples and cultures. However, organicist ideology takes the community as prior to individual interests, though it may make room for personal values. Mechanistic ideology stresses individual interests and capacities, viewing the community as an aggregation of particular interests.

The societal text of the Mackenzie Valley Pipeline Inquiry thus highlights the institutional patterns which generate these conflicting ideologies and the root metaphors which guide them. However, the foundations of these conflicting worlds are still obscure. The root metaphors furnish clues, but the symbolic horizons have yet to be disclosed. Since foundational symbols sustain and orient the totality of a people's world, they are lived through institutional patterns and projected in ideologies. However, it is the symbolic order that provides the backdrop against which institutions and ideologies can be evaluated. A merely subjective view of ideologies as projections of interest groups reduces the clash of ideologies to a struggle for power. This voluntaristic notion of ideology as merely the projection of collective will or interest is the stock in trade of mechanistic interpretations. In the mechanistic perspective, scientific and technological development is beyond ideology; hence, in this view, only peoples who have yet to enter the technological world of rational understanding and planning are subjects of ideology. Thus, mechanistic ideologies conceal their own ideological projections and symbolic foundations. They mask the spirituality of their corporate life and the life commitments which sustain it, viewing the communal claims and spirituality of other groups as sentimentality or nostalgia. Hence, the testing of ideologies and institutions requires a disclosure of the higher order symbols that found and orient them. Ideological clashes invite a hermeneutic of symbolic foundations, though they are often resolved through politico-economic or military force.

The mechanistic and organicist worlds are engaged in a deadly struggle of spiritual dimensions. Responsible decisions in this struggle require a disclosure of these spiritual, symbolic horizons. If there is to be a responsible, religious and moral decision about the future of Western peoples, not to speak of those other peoples whom they threaten, the hidden foundations of the techno-society will have to be revealed and evaluated in the light of authentic symbols of human dwelling.

The land is one of the centering symbols in the clash of worlds in the inquiry (Slater: chap. 3). The rallying cry of the native peoples of the North was initially about land claims. This was soon extended to include aboriginal rights, cultural autonomy, and political self-determination (Hutchinson). Symbols gather and center a world. They cluster with other symbolizations in an encompassing configuration. This has already been noted in Mircea Eliade's observation that symbols tend to system. Configuration is a better term, however, since centering illumines the power of symbol in human dwelling. It also expresses the fundamental notion of the symbolic ordering of the spatial world which Eliade traces in archaic symbolization (Eliade, 1959).

At the informal hearings in the North, local people revealed their sense of continuity through the land, of belonging within a world that is preserved and nourished by the land. This sense of spiritual identity with the land came out dramatically, if a bit harshly, in one of the hearings. Frank T'Seleie made the following remarks at the hearing in Fort Good Hope, 5 August 1975:

> Obviously Mr. Blair, president of Foothills (who is present) and his friend Mr. Horte, president of Gas Arctic, want to see us destroyed. Maybe Mr. Blair, that is because you do not know us or understand us. Or maybe money has become so important to

> you that you are losing your own humanity. . . . I only know you are a human being. There must be times when you too think of your children and their future. I doubt that you would knowingly destroy what is valuable to them. Why are you asking us to destroy our future? . . .
>
> Mr. Blair, there is a life and death struggle going on between us, between you and me. Somehow in your carpeted boardrooms, in your paneled office, you are plotting to take away from me the very centre of my existence. You are stealing my soul. Deep in the glass and concrete of your world you are stealing my soul, my spirit. By scheming to torture my land you are torturing me. By plotting to invade my land you are invading me. If you ever dig a trench through my land, you are cutting through me. . . .
>
> It seems to me that the whole point in living is to become as human as possible; to learn to understand the world and to live in it; to be part of it; to learn to understand the animals, for they are our brothers and they have much to teach us. We are a part of this world. [Watkins: 15f.]

The question of land for native people, as Frank T'Seleie expressed it so well, is where one centers human dwelling. Past and future, survival or destruction, a truly human way of life or the degradation of life, all of these dimensions of dwelling are gathered in the land for native peoples of the North. This is not to say that they despise or reject appropriate "development." That is a charge repeatedly made against them by representatives of the corporate interests. The reality is that they hope to accommodate such development to their communal bonding with the land rather than allowing their community life to be annihilated by the forces of development.

Land in a technologized world is merely a means for making money. Land is an exploitable, alienable resource. It can be bought and sold like any other commodity. It is rich in resources or barren. Land is a factor in the market like anything else—commodities, labor, capital. In the mechanistic paradigm, this is considered a "rational" approach to land, since land like anything else may be scarce in one place and plentiful in another. However, reduction of the land to a means for accumulation of capital conceals the spiritual realities on which the technological world is founded. This is the paradox of the technological order: it despises the higher order symbols of people who come under its sway, whether native peoples of the North or rural people who are not yet urbanized; meanwhile, it conceals its own spiritual foundations behind the mask of calculating rationality or practicality. Nevertheless, the higher order symbols of the techno-society are familiar to anyone raised within it, though they are taken for granted and repressed from consciousness. The central symbol is progress. Progress is expansion. The frontier or the underdeveloped nation is good because it is a place for extending human powers to develop, to advance, to conquer, to gain dominion, to increase control.

Other symbols cluster in this configuration. Individuality is the ultimate reality in this world, whether human individuality as interest or the individuality of entities such as land, goods, persons, or natural beings. Everything is what it is and not another thing. Techno-societies expend unlimited energies to save the life of a single individual trapped in a cave but consign whole populations to hunger and death on a principle of triage. Human rights are defended by techno-societies, but these are the rights of individuals in their system, not the rights of whole peoples. Progress, development, evolution, power as domination, freedom as autonomy—these and other symbolizations form the configuration of spiritual life in the techno-societies.

Land is a central symbolization for native peoples of the North, but power is the organizing symbol of the techno-society. Differences in the lived interpretations of power dramatize the conflict between the organicist heritage and the mechanistic age. Power among the Athapaskan Indians of the Northwest is a quality of relationship with the animals and spirits of their world.[3] In the hunting rituals, the powers inherent in the cosmos become manifest. Hunters participate in these powers and enter into communion with the animals they pursue (VanStone, chap. 4). This relational interpretation of power is lived out by all native peoples of the North so far as they have escaped the influence of the techno-society. In the techno-society, power is domination. It is power exercised by the stronger over the weaker, the technical expert over the ignorant, the corporate interests over local communities and economies. Power is imposition of the stronger will on the weaker. Power is hierarchical organization of life and activity by those who control capital, technology, and resources. The organicist heritage also celebrates hierarchy, but the hierarchy preserves the well-being of the parts. Organicist power is the quality of relations that pertain within that whole, maintaining bonds with earth and sky, mortals and immortals. By contrast, the symbolization of power in the mechanistic world sanctions autonomy, independence, invulnerability, and superiority.

The spirituality of the techno-society is at war with the spirituality of peoples in the organicist heritage who aspire to self-determination and sovereignty. This is the shape of the struggle for decolonization in the third world. Whether the colonization be political or economic, it expresses the ambition of the techno-society to subject all things to itself. This raises questions about the meaning of spirituality. Lust for domination seems anything but spiritual. However, the disfigurement of the human in the symbols of progress and domination illumines the ambiguity of spirituality and its vulnerability to distortion. Symbols conceal as well as reveal.

The religious heritage of the West is founded in a life commitment to a good creation. The biblical heritage identifies this creation with a divine source, the Lord of Creation. No matter how radically one interprets the Fall in the myths of creation, the symbolization of creation founds a triumph of good over evil, light over darkness, the powers of life over the powers of death (Kenick). In this respect, the symbols of cross and resurrection in the Christian story reiterate on an even deeper level that same affirmation of the goodness of creation and the union of power and goodness in the divine mystery. The goodness of life is also founded in the classical affirmation of Being as coming to be, unfolding powers of being (Heidegger, 1973). These strands converge in Western life and thought, affirming life and the creative powers of the human species. The techno-age inherited this life commitment to creation, though now it was alienated from a sense of the divine mystery. The dream of a rational society promised release from the domination of hierarchical authorities of church and state. The Western commitment to a good creation was thus displaced into the control of emerging industrial capitalism and the techno-age. The spirituality of this age is corrupt and distorted, yet it is founded in an authentic symbolization of the unity of goodness and power in the preservation and unfolding of life. Its spiritual task is the liberation of creation from the powers which now hold it in thrall.

This is the crisis of Western spirituality. Its spiritual heritage disfigures human dwelling. Its encounters with peoples like the Dene, not to speak of its confrontation with limits in the natural environment, threaten disaster. The spirit of mechanism holds the West in its power. Only a new image or paradigm can transcend an exhausted mechanism and integrate its hidden virtues with the communal solidarity of an historical, organicist legacy. Artistic process, I have been emphasizing, is just such a new paradigm of dwelling.

The confrontation of an exhausted techno-world with a communal world aspiring to new birth brings the hermeneutic full circle to the artistic paradigm. However, the challenge to the artistic metaphor is now on a much deeper level. Gadamer identified the historical character of human dwelling through the paradigm of the work of art. The question now arises as to the source of that history, the dynamic of a truly human history, the history to which underdeveloped nations and peoples aspire. The question remains as to how one determines an authentic rather than inauthentic symbolization of life. With all their promise, Western symbols have revealed their corruption. To transcend the crisis of Western spirituality and the imminent destruction of non-Western peoples, at least on the level of understanding and ideology, a new paradigm and spiritual foundation are required.

Paul Klee, I believe, unfolded such an interpretation as artistic process. He would probably not have phrased it in this way, yet his painting and reflections on artistic process disclose the foundations of human dwelling. His work synthesizes and orders mechanistic, organicist, and artistic paradigms in a way which promises transcendence of our present crisis.

Justice Thomas Berger recognized the place of transcending

judgment in dealing with the conflicting interpretations and perspectives in the hearings. In his words, "Indeed, when the main issue cuts across a range of questions, spanning the physical and social sciences, the only way to come to grips with it and to resolve it is by the exercise of human judgment" (Hutchinson and Winter). There is, of course, no way of avoiding human judgment. There are also grounds for judgment, some of which Justice Berger had employed. He concurred in the aspiration of the native peoples for self-determination, affirming this as a universal human claim. He considered the natural beauty and wildlife of the North as a precious heritage of all peoples. He respected the pressures to extend the supply of gas and oil to the South of Canada. He evinced uneasiness over the excessive consumerism of the Western world in relation to the developing areas (Berger, 1980). In brief, spiritual and moral commitments informed his judgments. The real question is how such judgments are founded. His opponents attributed these commitments to personal prejudice. They were in fact firmly grounded in a symbolic vision which is only now emerging in the struggles of Western society with its own, self-destructive tendencies. The conflict between corporate interests and traditional societies can be transcended in such a new vision, but neither mechanistic domination nor organicist solidarities can achieve such a transcendence. Hence, comprehension of the clash of worlds invites a retrieval of a more encompassing symbolic heritage and its conversion to an emerging, more human world. The artistic vision opens the way to such a retrieval and creative transformation.

ARTISTIC PROCESS AS CREATION

John Dixon identifies Paul Klee as the artist who expressed in words as well as works the new departure of modern art. Dixon identifies the emergence of modern art with founding figures such as Cézanne. He identifies this new departure by a definition of art "as the whole relation of humans to their world" and the disclosure of "the infinite variety of the human relation to the world" (Dixon: 141). Paul Klee delineates the dimensions of this new departure in a variety of styles and in works so rich that they defy classification. He also relocates the essence of the human within the natural process without surrendering the distinctively human role of making visible the invisible powers and forces of the world. Klee deepens the artistic paradigm in such a fashion that it functions as a paradigm of the theological imagination, giving us "a charter for the mode of theology that fits the imaginative structures of our day" (Dixon: 157). Thus, Paul Klee opens the way to go to the foundations of artistic process in creation.

Klee achieves a synthesis of root metaphors or paradigms in his work and thought. This synthesis is most evident in the organization of his *Notebooks* which formed his courses of instruction. He guides the student painstakingly through analytic work, tracing the dynamic forces of space and color. In this analytic work he stresses knowledge as well as sensibility, technique as well as imagination. He traces the movement of points, lines, planes, and figures, feeling the way with his students into the innermost forces of life and nature. He stresses rule and measurement, weight and rhythm, yet never at the cost of creative movement. He locates mechanistic forces in the context of creation as follows:

> "As creation is related to the creator, so is the work of art related to the law inherent in it." The work grows in its own way, on the basis of common, universal rules, but it is not the rule, not universal *a priori*. The work is not law, it is above law. . . . Art is a transmission of phenomenon, projection from the hyperdimensional, a metaphor for procreation, divination, mystery. [Klee, 1961: 59]

It is difficult to imagine a clearer sense of the dynamic infrastructure of natural forces, penetrating the corporeo-spatial tensions yet drawing them into the human universe.

As Paul Klee proceeds into his "Ways of Nature Study," the analytic work is articulated with genesis, growth, and the composition of form. The striking note throughout his writings, at least for one who is not an artist, is the stress on movement, dynamics, change, and creativity. The organicist imagery that runs through the *Notebooks* is set within this dynamism. He employs organicist imagery to integrate the analytic, mechanistic elements without obscuring their importance. He stresses the interplay of parts in the whole. This dialectical synthesis of mechanistic and organic processes is succinctly stated as follows:

> The aim of our theoretical work is always, in one form or another, the organization of differences into unity, the combination of organs into organism. . . . Likewise structure, which is what we are aiming at here, does not spring up ready-made but is developed from interior and exterior motifs into its parts and thence into a whole. [Klee, 1961: 449]

There is a bonding of inner and outward form through which the object grows. It is in this sense that Klee seems to use the word *essence*, meaning the inner way of being of what is, its way to be as a dynamic event. Thus he will say, "The organism is figured from within, on the basis of its essence" (Klee, 1961: 383). John Dixon notes that Klee conceived the ethical as continuous with the world of these dynamic forms, meaning that the ethical is the sense of essential movement. The forces of mechanism, thus, find their proper expression in the unfolding of form, in the appropriate way to be of what is. This reveals the sense of the archetypal in the dynamic process of creation, the proper way to be that is grasped in metaphor and mediated in symbol.

It is far from self-evident that artistic process is a creative transcendence, yet this is the center of Klee's vision. There have been mechanistic understandings of artistic process which subordinated art to the rule (Cassirer, 1951: chap. 7). Organicist interpretations of art dominated in the classical period even as mechanism took precedence in the modern age. John Dewey seems at times to move within this organicist imagery, though there are many indications that he had transcended it, converging with the sense of creation that marks Klee's higher synthesis (Dewey: 24f., 195, 272). With Paul Klee, there is no question that artistic process is the essentially human way of being within, yet transcending mechanistic forces and organicist forms. Even in his imagery of the creation of the work of art as the coming forth of fruit in the tree, Klee is affirming that the human is neither tree nor fruit but that power of seeing and thinking through which the fruit comes to be. The essentially human is the free, creative play that brings to light the play of creation. John Dixon explicates Klee's sense of creation most sensitively in his discussion of Klee's enchanting work "The Twittering Machine." How better to illumine the synthesis of mechanism and organicism in the free play of creation. As Klee observes, "The inner impulse is the urge that leads to production. As in nature, so with us, Nature is creative, and we are creative" (Klee, 1970: 259).

It would be misleading to systematize the synthesis of root metaphors or paradigms in Klee's work. He championed freedom and movement against rigid forms of any kind. The synthesis of paradigms in his *Notebooks* has rather the character of an endless movement, an endless dialectical motion from initial focus to new creation. He seems no sooner to have led his students through the painful struggle to grasp the geometrics of line, color, energy, and rhythm to the higher reaches of form and composition than he returns with the students to a new penetration of lines and forces. In his own words, "For the artist, dialogue with nature remains a *conditio sine qua non*. The artist is a man, himself nature and a part of nature in natural space." Creativity is not moving in an ideal space of forms but letting possibilities of form come to be in the human world. The human way to be is not something above nature or separate from nature. It is the intrinsically natural that is yet the fully and distinctively human.

In the language of hermeneutics, Klee fosters a hermeneutical circle that is thoroughly natural and human. The way of being within nature, a difficult task of feeling and thought, opens the way to the genesis of form, yet the form is free, nothing natural yet thoroughly nature. In this synthesis, Paul Klee discloses the human as image of God, liberating the symbol of creation that has been reduced to the analytic and geometric. One would seek far and wide in the humanities and sciences to find a more inspiring expression of this legacy of creation.

> Through the experience that he has gained in different ways and translated into work, the student demonstrates the progress of his dialogue with the natural object. His growth in the vision and contemplation of nature enables him to rise towards a metaphysical view of the world and to form free, abstract structures which surpass schematic intention and achieve a new naturalness, the naturalness of the work. Then he creates a work, or participates in the creation of works, that are the image of God's work. [Klee, 1961: 67]

This creative paradigm of art furnishes clues to life and thought in the crisis of Western spirituality. Paul Klee relocates human mind and life within nature without diminishing the transcendence of the human, whereas the mechanistic mind repudiates every attempt to go beyond instrumental rationality, challenging every transcendence as a return to the irrational or a flight into subjectivity. Klee demonstrates in his work and thought that the most thoroughgoing intellectual penetration and technical skill are the beginning and not the end of the creative process. He refuses to arrest this creative process in the achievement of form (Klee, 1961: 169).

The artistic paradigm, as illumined by Gadamer's work, is thoroughly historical. Paul Klee celebrated this sense of history without submitting the creative process to a dead past. History for Klee has a living quality that illumines and enriches. As he put it so well, the creative process moves "from prototype to archetype," never content to imitate tradition, yet learning from tradition to penetrate more deeply into the way things are (Klee, 1961: 93). To be located in nature as human is to be located historically, living out of the past through sensibility to the present into the creative possibilities of the future. The originary disclosures of the symbolic heritage come to be in this artistic process, undergoing transformative renewal as they are creatively appropriated.

This vision of nature and humanity synthesizes two dimensions of the human which have been at odds in Western history. The organicist heritage projected a hierarchical order of being to which the human is to be conformed, almost as a part of a natural order. This submissive, dependent image of the human fitted very well into the hierarchical orders of society in which this metaphor held sway. It also expressed the monarchical vision of a Creator God. The mechanistic vision of the Enlightenment upheld the powers of human rationality, liberating humanity from this hierarchical tradition. At the same time, mechanism projected a deterministic order to which the human would have to conform. Mechanism expressed an alienated vision of deity, aloof, detached, impassive. This submissive expression of mechanism persists, however, only in the realm of classical economics. Many economists still talk as though the rules of economic process were "nature's order," fixed, nonhistorical and nonhuman. If there be a deity, it would be deity as programmer.

However, mechanism gave rise to such powerful forces of science and technical development that modern forms of the megamachine entrust to professional elites the capacity to alter the structures of nature itself. Nuclear technology and genetic engineering are, in this sense, historical contradictions of the fiction of the laws of nature with which classical economics continues to operate. However, the submissive view of the organicist and the activist drive to domination of the latter day mechanist seem to miss the duality of true creativity. Paul Klee's vision reveals the human as receptive in its active creativity, creative and active in its receptivity. The human is productive and receptive at once, only becoming truly creative through its receptivity (Klee, 1961: 357). This suggests a proper role for science and technology in the new age. It can be the instrument for enriching human attunement to habitat and cosmos as well as a power for releasing and modifying natural forces. Paul Klee projects a servant image of the human in its truly creative movement of formation. This image transcends the struggle over the Mackenzie Valley pipeline, enlisting science and technology in the preservation rather than destruction of communities and environments.

Artistic process lets natural forces and forms come to light even as it transcends form through imagination. Klee's interpretation of artistic process centers the human reality in imagination. In John Dixon's proposal for the theological imagination, "If theology can understand what Klee did it might be better equipped to redo its own work. It is, in good part, the way, the process for the religious imagination" (Dixon: 142). Clearly this is the path that Paul Klee opens for the modern age. He makes visible the invisible powers of the human. He makes it clear, "We are human because we can know the metaphor," as Dixon puts it. Yet imagination is a most ambiguous power. Ever since Coleridge highlighted the importance of imagination, it has been understood as a human power pure and simple (Wheelwright, 1968: chap. 3). Most studies of imagination reveal this predilection to reduce imagination to a human power (Warnock: pt. 4). Thus, symbols and ideologies, science and technical achievements, the whole panoply of humanities and institutional arrangements can be assimilated to human ingenuity.

Paul Klee's work breaks with this subjectivist tradition. Once the receptive and productive aspects of human creativity are recognized, imagination is more appropriately interpreted as the attunement of the human to the creative process of bios and cosmos. Artistic process neither imposes form nor merely elicits form. Creative art attunes itself to natural forces and movements lending its own sensibility and creative grasp of the metaphor to make visible what is invisible. This is a mystery, the mystery of creation or cocreation in the image of the Creator's work. Klee is very clear on this. He points out that no amount of work can of itself produce creative work, even as creative work would not be possible without endless effort. This is the mystery of genius. It means that imagination is to be located neither in the subject nor in the object. Imagination is the peculiar attunement and sensibility in which the human and the natural are conjoined as creative process. Making visible archetypal directionalities and possibilities, knowing the metaphor, is participation in the divine artistry. This is the truly human work. This is the work of imagination, which is to say the relation of cocreator with the Creator in letting a world come to be.

This theology of creation in the dynamic sense of formation furnishes a clue to the meaning of truth in the new age. The mechanistic paradigm sought truth in the agreement of thought with fact. In scientific mechanism, truth is discovering the uniform in the changing, finding the rule. In technological mechanism, truth is reproducing through human operations the forces of nature. By contrast, the metaphysical truth of organicism is adequation of thought to reality. This tradition was discredited by the assaults of mechanism; hence, contemporary organicism falls back on dogmatism, tradition or assertion. Klee's artistic paradigm affirms the relative validity of these lower levels of truth. Attunement to forces and forms of nature is understanding receptivity; thus, truth is agreement of thought and technique with process. However, fully human truth is disclosure. In Klee's words, "Art does not reproduce the visible but makes visible" (Klee, 1961: 76). Truth is a letting come to be that reveals a world. Interpretations of truth as correspondence of thought and thing, adequation, or predictability presuppose this foundational truth of making visible or revealing. Mechanistic and organicist paradigms depend for their secondary truths upon the foundational truth of receptive/active creativity.

The artistic vision of creation discloses an historical horizon somewhat at odds with conventional Christianity. The Christian legacy is, to be sure, a plurality of many interpretations of the symbolic heritage. However, the weight of the tradition has been on the side of two histories: one spiritual, heavenly and eternal; the other earthly, corrupted by sin and destined to pass away. Augustine gave prototypical formulation to this mythology of the two histories in his classic work *The City of God,* juxtaposing the city of earth and the city of God, the one lost in sin, the other inviting the human to its eternal rest. The Augustinian vision drew upon a Neoplatonic heritage to appropriate eschatological motifs in the Christian narrative. His vision continues to be a dominant interpretation in the West. It gained a new lease in the Lutheran and Calvinist reforms. This myth of the two histories was challenged by a liberal vision of progress in the late nineteenth century, but World War I broke the spell of this liberal heritage.

The myth of two histories has recently been challenged again by liberation theology in Latin America, most notably in the pioneering work of Gustavo Gutierrez (Gutierrez). Many of the traditional symbols of the Christian heritage are radically transformed by claiming that there is one, divine-human history in which the saving power of grace is at work. Terms like *transcendence* take on a radically different meaning when the biblical affirmation of earthly history is recovered. Many biblical motifs support such an interpretation, but they have to be rescued from the two-story world of Neoplatonic metaphysics. One of the difficulties confronting liberation theology is the persistence of the metaphysical tradition amidst its own affirmations of the one divine-human history. The artistic vision of creation furnishes a paradigm within which the one history can be affirmed without repudiating the biblical symbols. It makes possible a liberation of creation as divine-human history. The divine creative process enjoys a transcendence of this one history, even as the human plays out its creative, transcending role amidst the forces and forms of nature. Creation discloses but does not exhaust the divine life. Martin Buber glimpsed this transformative and redemptive sense of creation in his exposition of Hasidism:

> Let us, the Hasidic rabbi says to the world, prepare for God a dwellingplace into which He desires to enter; when it is prepared by us, by the world of its own will—we let God in. The hallowing of the world will be this letting-in. But grace wants to help the world to hallow itself. . . . Man cannot approach the divine by reaching beyond the human; he can approach Him through becoming human. [Buber, 1958: 35, 42f.]

The sacrality of history, its authentic truth, is the quality of receptive, creative work of divine grace in human dwelling.

The artistic vision of creation founds the historical horizon as a divine-human work. Religious traditions have generally tended to dogmatize a particular symbolization as a final revelation. This has been particularly true of Western religious traditions, a trait which has supported imperialism in recent centuries. Every kind of evil from enslaving Africans to genocide against native peoples of the Americas found ideological support in Christian absolutism. But the artistic vision affirms creation without such absolutes or dogmas. It affirms a divine-human history as open, pluralistic, and creative. This means that the originary symbolic disclosures of various peoples, cultures, and traditions participate in the divine-human history. The one history belongs to a plurality of peoples and faiths. These histories may vary in their symbols, myths, rituals, politico-economic arrangements, and communal traditions but they all belong to the one history as copartners in creation. Sacral history is, then, an ecumenical, pluralistic history of peoples and cultures, each meriting respect and each learning from others through mutual dialogue. If one takes ecumenical in its true meaning as universal, not merely multiple expressions of the Christian heritage, then divine-human history is one, ecumenical history of creation to which every people and culture can contribute creatively. This is not to say that all faiths are the same or even equally adequate to the full richness of creation. It only says that the creative process is the true way of being of all peoples. Only they can determine the path of their fulfilment.

Western Christianity contributed to the bondage of creation under industrial capitalism. It elevated the Fall to a dogmatic concept of Original Sin, undercutting the creative powers of human life and consigning history to the megamachine (Ricoeur, 1974: 269–86). The myth of the Fall has its place in the story of creation. Those who have lived through the blood bath of the twentieth century do not have to be told that evil is a powerful force in history. The spirituality of corporate life may become distorted, wreaking destruction on the powerless. An artistic vision of creation is fully capable of comprehending the forces of evil without relegating history to alien powers. The liberation of creation discloses the power of divine love and justice to transform the destructive forces which human freedom makes possible. This sense of rupture in creation is recognized by Klee without consigning the world to alien powers:

> Man's ability to measure the spiritual, earthbound and cosmic, set against his physical helplessness; this is his fundamental tragedy. The tragedy of spirituality. The consequence of this simultaneous helplessness of the body and mobility of the spirit is the dichotomy of human existence.

> Man is half a prisoner, half borne on wings. Each of the two halves perceives the tragedy of its halfness by awareness of its counterpart. [Klee, 1961: 407]

The distorted spirituality of the techno-society reveals this tragedy all too well—an infinite drive to increase dominion conceals earthly creatureliness, threatening its own destruction through the very acquisition of power. The biblical heritage among others affirms the ultimate power of the divine mystery over every evil force. This is the heart of the biblical affirmation of the oneness of God. In the artistic vision, the divine mystery dwells also in the duality of creative power and limitation, the limitation of the divine love or what Abraham Heschel spoke of as the "pathos of God" (Heschel). Even in the divine self-limitation of receptive love, creation is at work bringing good out of evil, Shalom out of chaos and confusion.

Paul Klee's artistic vision grew out of his work and effectively transformed his teaching and work, giving it its rich originality. The same holds for the religio-ethical vision that emerges from a liberation of creation. The retrieval of the creational symbolism is potentially a transformation of the present age. The retrieval of creation as foundational symbolism is arising from imminent threats to the created world and its creatures. Reflective interpretations, when they are more than a spectator sport or academic exercise, arise in such conflicts of praxis and unfold in a transformed praxis. The resymbolization of the present age will inform and empower a creative praxis or it will perish along with the many species of life that are now being driven from the earth by rampant mechanism.

A TRANSFORMATIVE INTERPRETATION OF CREATION

Returning to the paradigmatic struggle over the Mackenzie Valley pipeline in the context of a resymbolization of creation, the proposals of the Berger inquiry take on a special importance. The inquiry recommended, as noted above, a ten-year moratorium on building and strengthening of the native economy of renewable resources. It also specified, in a second volume, conditions for protecting the environment, limiting the impact of economic development in the future and protection of land, wildlife, rivers and streams. The societal conditions of the native people of the North are safeguarded, yet the claims of the techno-society of the South are respected. The ethical note is sounded repeatedly in the inquiry. The ethical concern is spelled out in specific policies and strategies for an appropriate praxis. In his introduction to the second volume, Justice Thomas H. Berger articulates this ethical concern without equivocation:

> The condition of native people in the North today is, in many respects, the product of white domination of native people and native society. That this domination has often been benevolent does not at all diminish its devastating consequences for the patterns of collective and cooperative self-reliance that are the tradition of northern native people. Despite the benefits that the dominant white society has brought to native people—benefits that they readily acknowledge—this dominance, and the resulting weakness of their own society, have left native people, as a group, and as individuals, especially vulnerable to the impact of large-scale industrial development. [Berger, 1977: vol. 2, xi]

It would be inappropriate to trace in detail the strategies proposed in the inquiry. That is a task for Canadian people of the South and native people of the North as they work through their common future. However, the resymbolization of creation discloses the implicit foundation for a common rather than mutually destructive future. Furthermore, the artistic paradigm as a vision of creation offers some guidelines for the preservation of environments, communities and public life. These concerns touch communities throughout the techno-societies and in the third world. In this respect, the struggle of the native people of the North of Canada reflects struggles of all human communities against the juggernaut of the techno-machine age.

The spirituality of the techno-society centers in two symbols that represent a distortion of the Western symbolization of the good creation. The symbol of progress transformed a biblical interpretation of the fulfillment of creation in a redeemed kingdom into infinite human progress through mastery of the world.

The symbolization of power as imposition of human will transformed the biblical symbol of the human in the image of God to the human in the role of a monarchical ruler. The resymbolization of creation opens the way to a critique of these distortions in Western spirituality.

Infinite progress or development is a paradoxical interpretation of a biblical heritage which stressed the finitude of human life. However, the radical transcendence of the monarchical deity of Calvinist theology seems to have relegated earthly history to the mastery of the saints and ultimately to mastery by industrial capitalism. This suggests an inversion of the Weberian thesis. Max Weber argued that uncertainty over one's election to salvation led the pious to a life of discipline, frugality, and accumulation in order to gain assurance of salvation. This motivation undergirded the emergence of rational capitalism (Weber, 1958). Weber's thesis could then be restated: the impetus to mastery, deeply etched in Western life from classical times and held in check by the church, was released by a theology of radical transcendence and consignment of the world to the saints. Once the drive to mastery was released, the course of creation could be reinterpreted as a human project with an infinite future.[4] In this perspective, economic imperialism and unlimited exploitation of land, resources and labor were logical consequences of the preemption of the divine role in creation. The sense of progress emerged slowly in this vision of human mastery, though it is already present in the thought of Francis Bacon, the prophet of the techno-age. Progress is in many ways a displacement into history of biblical hope for a final dénouement in the struggle of the Creator against the powers of darkness. Thus, the symbol of progress, as well as its corollaries in theories of development, represents an historical distortion in the symbol of creation. The truth in this interpretation is evident in the sense of historical responsibility. The distortion lies in its disregard of the natural creation and the limits that belong to nature and humanity. The artistic vision of creation relocates this creative drive within nature.

Commitment to unlimited progress undoubtedly finds its deeper dynamic in the symbolization of power as mastery and domination. The biblical image of monarchical rule is a concealment in the revelation of the divine mystery. It is not the only symbolism of the divine and it is certainly an inappropriate image in a modern historical world (Migliore). The interplay of power and powerlessness, creativity and receptivity, active love and suffering pathos, reflects much more fully the inner spirit of the Hebrew scriptures, as Abraham Heschel and others have observed (Heschel). The pathos of the Creator is further disclosed in the Christian symbols of the cross and love of neighbor. This is a relational interpretation of power which includes vulnerability. Power as control has value in the relative place of mechanistic forces, but it has no claim to priority over the rhythms of nature, the health of communities, or the well-being of peoples. The artistic vision of creation refers mechanistic and relational powers to the higher purpose of enhancing and enriching human life and meanings. In creation, the quality of human dwelling takes priority over every exercise of human control or collective interest. In this sense, the artistic paradigm affirms yet relativizes both mechanistic and organicist interpretations of the symbolization of power.

The centrality of power in human history raises the question of the place of confessional faiths in this historical age of one, ecumenical history of many peoples and faiths. If the quality of dwelling reveals the sacred, then all regions of life are places for celebration of the mystery. The sacred realm is not confined to a church or a hierocratic Christendom. There is one history which the divine mystery shares with humanity. What, then, is the role of confessional communities which bear the heritages of Christian, Jewish, Islamic, Buddhist, and other faiths?

Power is the common ground and source of difference for the confessional and political communities. The systematic distortion of power relations is the way in which injustice appears in human dwelling. That distortion is rooted in symbolism itself. The symbol mediates the otherness of persons, communities, and the divine mystery. Such transcending otherness confronts humanity with its limits, its lack of final power over its own possibilities. By the same token, the mediation of otherness lures humanity into the struggle to overcome its limits, to become arbiter of the future by dominating its world. This is the ambiguity which Paul Klee identified as the oscillation between power and powerlessness. In the interplay of receptivity and activity, the temptation is to reject receptivity for an active exercise of power, to reject relational, dialogic power for controlling, monologic power. Both confessional and political communities have been drawn into such systematic distortions in the course of history. Nevertheless, confessional communities are called to be witnesses to the receptivity of the creature in the exercise of power. Political communities are called to active power in the exercise of responsibility for the preservation and enhancement of justice and peace. The prophetic task of the confessional communities is often costly and is symbolized in the Christian heritage by the cross. The responsibility of the political community may be equally costly as symbolized in Abraham Lincoln's Second Inaugural Address and his assassination. The dialectic between these communities is ontologically grounded in creation, for partnership in the work of creation involves the possibility of taking possession of creation. This is the possibility that is being attempted in the technological project. The prophetic task of the confessional communities confronts this project in the escalating arms race, the violation of the rhythms of nature, the destruction of peoples and communities, and the injustices that accompany the extension of power as domination. The confessional communities in Canada undertook the prophetic task in the struggle of the native people of the North of Canada through Project North, a ministry to empower people in their struggle for liberation. This is not the only task of confessional communities, since they are the bearers of the symbolic heritage of creation and redemption, but preserving that heritage and witnessing to its power for justice are one and the same. This is the costly truth that the church in Latin America has proclaimed since the meeting of the bishops at Medellin. But, in each instance, a confessional faith is charged with the preservation and interpretation of the legacy of symbols through teaching, story, ritual, and communal life. The basic task of confession is the empowering of people for their own history.

The artistic paradigm also furnishes clues to strategies for a future that transcends the exploitation of the techno-society and the vulnerability of native peoples. Again, the details of strategy fall to those engaged in a particular struggle, but the resymbolization of creation offers some helpful guidelines.

One can only admire the wisdom of the strategic proposals of the Berger inquiry. Establishing conditions for building the pipeline, limiting intrusion of workers from the outside, care of the ranges of renewable resources and protection of endangered species are all touched upon in the proposals. However, the economic power of the corporate interests remains untouched. To be sure, an inquiry that is commissioned to examine social and economic impact is hardly in a position to propose a transformation in the Canadian economy. Nevertheless, the inquiry affirmed the importance of self-development by the native people of the north if they were to survive. This does not seem possible so long as corporate economic powers are developing gas and oil resources in the North. The Canadian government owns these resources, to be sure, and could control development in principle. However, the actual development and control of Canadian resources fall largely to economic interests in the United States.[5] There is no reason to assume that these corporate interests will pay any more attention to local communities and their self-determination in the future than they have in the past.

There is every reason to assume within the artistic paradigm that the energies which constitute the infrastructure should be subject to the forms appropriate to the totality. In human dwelling, this implies that economic and technological forces should fall under the direction of the political representatives who preserve a people's future. This is quite evident in the paradigm drawn in figure I (p. 45) which diagrammed the dimensions of artistic process. The organizing agency of the work of art has to respect the rhythms of the energies that collaborate in the work, but the emergence of appropriate forms would be bizarre if they were determined by the infrastructure. Industrial capitalism has claimed just such autonomy for its economic interests. In the present stage of its development, transnational, corporate capitalism is moving toward global domination. There seems to be no possibility of bringing these autonomous powers to a position of historical responsibility unless resource development is nationalized and economic power is socialized (Barnet). This may take various forms, as is already the case in various parts of the world. However, development of any energy corridor in the Mackenzie Valley, as the case in point, for the profit of national and transnational corporate capitalism can only spell disaster for the native people of the North and ultimately for Canada's future. How much local, self-determination can enter into any such development, should it occur at all, remains a practical political issue between the native people and the government of Canada. However, something like a communitarian socialism which maximized local autonomy and control would seem to be the most appropriate expression of the dynamics of the artistic paradigm. Only political agency can regard the justice of the people, harmonizing the energies and rhythms of the infrastructure of dwelling. This is the truth which capitalism violates.

The artistic vision also discloses the ethical quality of dwelling. Paul Klee referred to this as the inner way of being of what appears, its essential movement (Klee, 1961: 444). This ethical quality reflects the archetypal directionalities informing all natural and human processes. On the human level, these directionalities are fluid. They are open to various forms of creative expression. They do, nevertheless, reflect the deeper flow of human energies and rhythms. They are not random. The human is not infinitely plastic. The native people of the North repeatedly point to these deeper bonds with nature and one another, mourning their destruction wherever the amoral and alienating forces of the industrial economy have intruded. Patterns of dwelling never fully embody the possibilities of such directionalities, since they are not eternal forms which could be discerned and imposed like a "natural" order.

However, some modes of dwelling unfold these possibilities more adequately than others. Industrial capitalism broke radically with traditional modes of preserving human dwelling, promising to raise human life to undreamed-of heights of affluence and ease when left to its own devices. The result has been erosion of community and spreading hunger. By contrast, the traditions of the native people of the North, as of all village peoples who have survived over thousands of years, furnish clues to an ethical way of dwelling which preserves life. These clues can be discerned more easily in the artistic paradigm than in either mechanistic or organicist interpretations, for the techno-age has created insuperable difficulties for the survival of organicist communities.

The overarching symbol for the ethic of dwelling is justice. In biblical terms, the righteousness of the mystery is the power to life. On the political level, justice emerges as the creative responsibility of a people for its history, including the control of its economic life for the preservation of all species life and the well-being of future generations. Justice in the economic realm, especially in its bearing on human communities, has important implications for a human future. These are ethical concerns that bear on any strategy affecting native people of the North. Some dimensions of this ethic of dwelling reveal the imperatives that are implicit in a vision of creation.

The preservation of species life involves protection of the environment and provision for the economic needs of people. These needs are being ignored or violated in almost every land that has felt the impact of industrial capitalism. They are the simple needs for adequate food, shelter, energy, and health care. The spread of industrial capitalism violates these basic needs, bringing hunger and unemployment to lands and peoples who had never known such deprivation (Barnet).

The preservation of species life also involves the health of human communities. This differs from health care of persons and families, though the two are closely interwoven. The health of human communities was learned by trial and error through the ages. Industrial capitalism undermined this wisdom and the communities it had preserved. The growth of bureaucracies of health, education, and welfare has often contributed to the dependency of peoples and the decay of communities. The escalation of crime and drugs in urban areas also reflects this decay of community. Little is remembered of the wisdom of peasant peoples about the preservation of healthy communities, though the native people of the North rehearsed that wisdom in the informal hearings. Much is being learned now about healthy environments and the dangers of polluting streams and oceans, atmosphere and soils with chemicals, nuclear waste and effluents of all kinds. Much has yet to be learned about the health of human communities, their stability and inner bonds of support and integrity. Moreover, racial, sexist, and social-class oppressions violate community in the United States and other countries. However, the furtherance of standards of justice in all of these realms depends ultimately on the fashioning of healthy communities. Standards of open access, equal rights and minimal standards of life do not threaten healthy communities but ultimately make them possible. It has been the conspiracy of industrial capitalism and its governmental collaborators to undermine equal rights and minimal standards in the name of a mythical freedom of opportunity. The ghettoization of urban areas in the United States has been the result of such a conspiracy.

Another ethical aspect of the essential way of being of dwelling is a participatory society. The native people of the North have insisted repeatedly that their government, education of their children, economic life, and communal integrity have been undermined by the imposition of alien governmental administration. The artistic vision emerges with a creative age of human responsibility for history. People are the creative agents of their history. Such creativity reveals the essence of the human in the image of God. This implies ownership and management of their own economic activities. Whatever values accrued from the wage economy of industrial capitalism, its mechanisms have to be brought into the orbit of a participatory society. However important the fashioning of an adequate politics on the macro-level to deal with the transnational corporate powers, there is need for a simultaneous rebuilding or building of local political participation and responsibility.

The Berger inquiry pointed to some of these ethical aspects within the limited mandate of its commission. The native people of the North made their claims for justice in these and other ways. The artistic vision only illumines the central importance of the ethical in the essential movement of any artistic work. That ethical quality is of the very essence of human dwelling in all regions of its activity. But, whatever is said in these reflective interpretations or the proposals of the Berger inquiry, the real risks and decisions of praxis fall to the various interests that converge in the Mackenzie Valley. Objectivity in inquiries does not come with reduction to a mechanistic identification of forces. This was the claim of the economists who challenged the Berger inquiry. Objectivity comes in the human community where people gain a voice and are heard. The human community dwells through its symbols and interpretations. The monologic forces of the techno-society strive to silence such voices in order to extend domination. The Berger inquiry achieved the true objectivity of human understanding—hearing, listening and heeding, especially where the silenced peoples of the colonialized regions can be heard in their own tongues and on their own terms. These reflections on their declaration only have merit so far as they point to the universal character of their aspirations and the relevance of their claims for the suffering of peoples throughout the world.

RELIGIOUS SOCIAL ETHICS

This exploration of the foundations of religious social ethics began with the crisis engendered by the mechanistic age. It has concluded with an artistic vision of creation that can transcend mechanism yet retain its valid elements. This is the hope of all those who recognize that modern technology has become almost indispensable to human survival. Whether creation can be liberated from the bondage imposed by mechanism will depend upon the praxis of peoples who face the deeper contradictions of the techno-society. The role of religious social ethics, the kind of inquiry that has been pursued in this study, is to help in raising some of these issues and possibilities. However, there are conflicting views of the discipline and much misunderstanding about its character. By way of conclusion it may be useful to delineate the nature and task of the discipline.

Religious social ethics is a hermeneutic of the historical

dwelling of peoples. This is the understanding of the discipline that follows from an artistic paradigm. People dwell poetically and symbolically on the earth. Their dwelling lives the symbols that found their world. Their interpretations unfold and transform those symbols, constituting an historical identity as a people. The Dene, for example, are moving toward a new way of life, yet trying to retain valid elements in the old ways. The Women's Movement in the United States is striving to achieve justice in legal, economic, political, and communal relationships. At the same time, it is trying to hold to valid feminine interests and modes of action. Where the mechanistic pattern of working relationships is one of manipulation without feeling, many women find mutuality of concern and open exchange of thoughts a more appropriate way of working. The pressures of a mechanistic society draw women into the alienating pattern, yet their aspirations for equal rights include the right to work and act according to their more humane style. Hence, the symbolization of the human is being challenged and transformed by women's struggle for justice in the techno-society. Symbols are lived, yet they are constantly undergoing transformative influences. This is the dynamic process that religious social ethics attempts to understand and illumine.

Ideology furnishes the subject matter of religious social ethics, for ideology expresses a people's struggle with power and its hope for the future. Since ideology conceals social realities while also projecting a model for the future, ideologies become important indicators of historical struggles. Some of the dimensions of ideology have already been considered in chapter 3. However, the pervasive character of ideology creates special problems for ethical inquiry. The very fact that every ideology involves some masking of reality implies that every ideology requires unmasking. But even more serious is the fact that all thought bears an ideological taint, because all thought arises from and contributes to human life and its projects. Even the seemingly factual studies of history are bound up with significance for human life (Gadamer: 303). This suggests that the disciplines that constitute religious social ethics are all, in some respects, ideologically qualified.

The human sciences are ideological, since they involve assumptions about how and why people act, thus projecting some model for a human future. They are also ideological insofar as they involve prejudgments about what is important in societal process, highlighting some aspects of social reality and obscuring other elements. Furthermore, the human sciences are essentially historical sciences within the artistic paradigm, since human dwelling is historically constituted by symbol and interpretation. A nonhistorical interpretation of such an historical process would be an ideological concealment of the true dynamics of dwelling. Nevertheless, the human sciences can contribute to the understanding of societal process and constitute an essential ingredient of any ethical inquiry.

Furthermore, moral or ethical sciences are ideological in that they project a model for right action or social justice. They are also ideological in that they are bearers of moral codes that legitimate the power structure of a society. Debates over human rights in foreign policy reflect this ideological taint in ethics and politics. From 1976 to 1980 the Carter administration stressed human rights in its dealings with other nations. The Reagan administration reversed this policy in February 1981, recommending an ethicist, Ernest W. Lefever, as Assistant Secretary for Human Rights, after he argued that authoritarian regimes should not be sanctioned for abuses of human rights. (The recommendation was rejected by a Senate committee and Lefever withdrew from consideration.) In both instances, the policies involved ethical, political, and ideological elements. Moral, ethical, and political proposals involve an implicit or explicit ideology of human fulfillment.

Theology is the most thoroughly ideological of all cultural disciplines, for theology proposes an understanding of the human condition in its proximate and ultimate possibilities. Theologies have often claimed a monopoly on "really" understanding the human predicament and prescribing for its future. The Moral Majority took this ideological task to its bosom in 1980, determining what was right for women, children, and welfare recipients (Falwell). However, all theologies involve implicit or explicit proposals for action, for fulfillment of human life. The liberation theologians of Latin America have been self-conscious in developing their ideologies, affirming without hesitation that faith involves commitments in social, economic, political, moral, and spiritual terms. In fact, liberation theologians have criticized their more academically oriented colleagues for refusing to face the ideological implications of their institutional involvements and commitments, for refusing to recognize their ideological complicity with oppression. To refuse political responsibility is already to make a choice to support the established powers which, in the perspective of liberation theology, are oppressing peoples throughout the world.

Religious social ethics seems destined to be one more contribution to this cacophony of ideologies. If such an ethic could draw on a simply empirical social science, there might be a way through the morass of ideologies. However, this is not the case, despite the claims of a value-free human science. If moral reflection could achieve a determinate understanding of the right and the just, such an ethic might provide clear guidelines for human action. However, social morality is always the morality of the established powers in a society, imposing an order that preserves the authority of those in power over against the underprivileged and oppressed. The most obvious example in the United States is the sacred right of private property which preserves the ownership of most of America's wealth by very few, excluding the mass of the population from any property in land or capital. The same holds for the right of equal opportunity which is used to oppose affirmative action programs as in the Bakke case, where a white man charged discrimination when minority groups were being given special consideration. The principle of equal opportunity presupposes equal power and equal access, but women, black men, and minority groups do not enjoy either equal power or equal access; consequently, the moral principle serves as an ideology to conceal the inequalities of the society and to preserve the advantages of those who benefit from them. Similar ideological limitations confront the theological disciplines. The religious symbols which constitute the foundations of theological inquiry are inextricably interwoven with the original social stratum that bears the symbols.

Theology, like the human and moral sciences, is an ideological expression of proposals for personal fulfillment in the context of universal fulfillment.

Perhaps root metaphors or paradigms could liberate religious social ethics from this babel of ideologies. The foregoing inquiry has demonstrated that such metaphors operate at the interface of symbol and interpretation, guiding lived interpretations in their appropriation of symbols and furnishing clues to a transformation of symbols. Unfortunately, the root metaphors or paradigms bear an ideological taint. This taint is, perhaps, more a *tilt,* to use a term that has gained a certain currency in foreign policy. Organicist thinking leans to hierarchical order, since it starts with the whole and treats the parts as functions within that totality. At the same time, there are many different appropriations of the organicist metaphor, so that a wide range of understandings of human fulfillment may draw on a similar metaphor. The organicist cosmology of Egypt drew upon the regular rhythm of the flooding of the Nile as a model of an orderly, harmonious pattern of life under the pharoah of the two kingdoms. By contrast, the organicist cosmology of Mesopotamia projected a mood of radical conflict in religious and political life. A similar case can be made for mechanism. The mechanistic metaphor tilts toward domination and exercise of force in achieving social order. Thomas Hobbes developed his mechanistic understanding of society in this fashion. John Locke developed a more sanguine view of human action from a similar paradigm, arguing for a limited rather than encompassing state. Similarly, the Federalist theory took its departure in a mechanistic paradigm, arguing that the very conflict of forces required a democratic process in which such forces could be balanced.

The artistic paradigm tilts toward a dialogical, even dialectical process of creation and transformation. Art is closest to the political theory of perpetual revolution. Nothing detracts from art so much as mechanical repetition. The ideological tilt is toward a participatory order that is open to criticism, challenge, and transformation. Artistic process thrives upon freedom of expression. There are, of course, many interpretations of the artistic paradigm ranging from the simple craft understanding to the elitist art of genius to the understanding of artistry as the creativity of the human. The last interpretation has informed the preceding inquiry and indicates the ideological bent of these reflections. In every instance, the historical world reveals itself as projecting one or another understanding of human order and fulfillment, one or another ideological possibility.

This poses the question of achieving some kind of consensus on a more just, more humane, and more ultimately promising direction for life and action. Religious social ethics is essentially a critique and proposal of ideology. It is critique of false consciousness. It is proposal of an authentic future. In what way is this possible in view of the ideological character of its constitutive disciplines?

The model for reading a text furnishes an order within which religious social ethics can effect a helpful critique as well as proposal of ideologies. Once it is acknowledged that the guess, the root metaphor, already lends an ideological tilt, then every claim to value-free proposals can be dismissed. The only question is which proposal furthers the struggle for justice and public happiness. No proposal can be fully adequate to the possibilities for social justice, since every proposal is located somewhere in social space and is, thus, discriminatory in some respects.

Taking artistic process as the most promising guess for a critique and proposal of ideology in contemporary society, the role of human science, ethics, and theology in religious social ethics can be delineated.

The critique of ideology involves a hermeneutic of suspicion, an attempt to deconstruct a prevailing ideology in order to trace the interests that sustain it and the societal realities which it conceals. The human sciences have contributed most significantly to this aspect of religious social ethics since their inception. This is an explanatory task in bringing the guess concretely to a specific event. For example, the return of the hostages during Ronald Reagan's inauguration in January of 1981 brought into play various ideological dynamics which can be traced in an explanatory sequence. This is a critical function of social science. It is indispensable to ethics and theology in pursuing their work.

The homecoming of the American hostages from Iran demands ideological interpretation. It expressed a ground swell of feeling and enthusiasm that shocked even the political leaders who hoped to benefit from it. The symbolizations of the event were filled with nostalgia for the old days—homecoming, restoration, and return. Moreover, home, family, local community, church, and nation, all played a part in the rituals and symbolic configuration. This was a celebration of the civil religion in its various forms of family, church, and country.

The human sciences are eminently qualified to locate the dynamic forces that generated this celebration. They have developed analytic tools for understanding the forces at play in social process. Certain of these forces stand out for any critical analysis. The United States had not only been embarrassed by the taking of the hostages but had found itself powerless to effect their release. This international attack on American prestige was only one of a series of difficulties following upon defeat in Viet Nam. In addition, the civil rights struggles of recent years failed to effect major improvements in the condition of the poor and minorities, and the society found itself more divided, if anything, than before the struggle. Furthermore, the economic pressures of inflation, unemployment, and deindustrialization were creating uncertainties about the American future. In addition, American family and home life have suffered radical dislocation with the massive entrance of women into the labor force and the threats to traditional family patterns that have come with the Women's Movement. The Moral Majority had for some months been driving home this sense of crisis as the traditional form of the nuclear family was shrinking to about fifteen percent of American families. And, finally, local communities were experiencing the erosion of any decision-making power in matters affecting their destinies, whether in retaining industry in their areas or in altering national policies shaping local conditions. These and other forces entered into the explosion of nationalistic feeling at the homecoming. In this phase of the critique of ideologies, the human sciences are indispensable even though they bring their own prejudices to any such analysis.

Ethical reflection enters into critique of ideology on the boundary between explanatory understanding and comprehension of the symbols that empower the ideology. In this respect, ethical thought operates between human science and theology, between the tracing of social dynamics and the interpretation of encompassing symbols. This can be clarified by considering, once again, the ideological event of the return of the hostages. The homecoming covered over the role of the United States in restoring the Shah to power in Iran in 1954. Thus, the celebration pushed into the background any awareness of American complicity in the despoiling of the wealth of Iran and the oppression of its people. Moreover, the jubilation over the hostages successfully passed over the women and black hostages who had been released early by the authorities in Iran. In addition, Viet Nam veterans were left more intensely aware than ever that their country rejected their sacrifice and intended to ignore their postwar sufferings. (By 1980 the number of suicides among returned veterans of Viet Nam had exceeded the number of fatalities suffered in Viet Nam itself.[6]) This rejection of the Viet Nam veterans was highlighted by the excess of jubilation over the return of the hostages. There are, of course, other ethical dimensions to the critique of this ideological event, but these are indications of the role of moral reflection in this critique. Moral reflection as critique of ideology discloses the injustices that are covered by ideology, bringing its own ethical assumptions under critique as part of the public ideology. Thus, ethics draws upon social analysis, yet opens on the symbolic horizon of justice and public happiness for its critical understanding. There is no possibility of moral critique of ideology except in the context of some encompassing symbolization of justice. Ethics is, then, human science raised to the level of moral reflection. It is, by the same token, philosophical and theological reflection on symbols brought into the context of praxis.

Philosophical and theological critique of ideology moves within the moment of comprehension of the text, interpreting the symbolic horizon within which the ideology functions. Ideologies, as was noted in chapter 3, unfold the symbolic foundations of tradition and open out upon a symbolic horizon of a people's hope for fulfillment. Theology, to take one of the major disciplines in a critique of ideology, only has access to such symbolic horizons through the work of human science and ethics. A theology that works simply from its symbolic legacy runs the danger of being abstract manipulation of doctrines, displaced from its true home in the praxis of the one, ecumenical history of human dwelling. Theology, in this sense, is dependent upon the human sciences for its grasp of the forces playing into ideological proposals, including its own ideological expressions. By the same token, theology depends upon moral inquiry to clarify its complicity in the injustices of society and to illumine the symbolization of justice which locates faith in praxis. Theology is a critique of ideology, but its special function in that critique is the disclosure of the symbolic horizons that control the ideology. The celebration of the return of the hostages lifted up the sacred quality of family life, homecoming, religious faith, and loyalty to one's nation and people. At the same time, these symbols were being abused for the sake of concealing the destructive forces of the techno-society. The hermeneutic of symbols in turn illumines for ethics and the human sciences the broader dimensions of a particular ideological event or proposal. Ethics cannot rest simply with the symbolization of justice, for every interpretation of justice presupposes some broader vision of the human project. Similarly, the human sciences operate blindly amidst the complex forces of society unless they can grasp the moral struggles that move peoples. Religious social ethics is, thus, the disciplined inquiry of a community of those who are committed to the struggle for justice and peace. The critique of ideology is the central task of such a community. It can only be advanced by communication within these specialized disciplines whose true nature is defined by this common task.

The proposal of ideology or hermeneutic of transformation reverses the sequence of the critique. Creative ideology opens up a direction toward justice amidst injustice, peace amidst war. In this respect, its foundations are disclosed in a retrieval of authentic symbolization amidst symbolic distortions. This is the constructive task of theology, the retrieval of the originary symbolizations of its heritage in the light of the transforming claims of the new situation in which the struggle for justice is pursued. In the return of the hostages, this resymbolization would involve opening the Shalom of the mystery amidst the deepest anxieties that generated the celebration, the anxiety of nuclear annihilation which the techno-society has imposed on peoples throughout the world. It also involves founding a liberated family life, restoration of local communal life, building of an economy that ministers to human needs and recovery of a nationalism that preserves rather than endangers life. These and other aspects of creative ideology require a retrieval of sound symbolic foundations. There is no untainted symbolic heritage to which theology can go in order to disclose such a horizon. Its hermeneutic work involves grasping what was concealed in the heritage itself and disfigured in the course of history. This is a creative, poetic work of discernment in the context of contemporary struggles. The horizon of possibilities projected by the tradition can thus be fused with the horizon of the struggle for justice and liberation.

Ethical inquiry depends upon the theological retrieval of symbolic foundations for its creative contribution to ideology. The formulation of ethical policies and strategies of action requires some sense of the appropriate action (Ogletree). The idea of the fitting is a proper way to understand a hermeneutical approach to ethics, but the sense of the fitting presupposes a world to which it is fit. Human interests and consciousness are much too limited to furnish a horizon of the fitting. In this sense, ethics implicitly or explicitly draws upon a theological hermeneutic of symbols in its prescriptive task. The symbols furnish the horizon within which judgments of the fitting can be made.

The human sciences contribute to a creative ideology by forging policies and strategies for social transformation. Such policies presuppose a moral judgment as to imperatives for action that will contribute to the public happiness. To this extent, the human sciences depend upon theology and ethics when they enter constructively upon the work of policy. This may occur without reflection, but every policy that proposes a human future involves one or another decision about the right and the good. The creative moment of explanation in reading the text thus becomes the moment of practical construction to which theology, ethics, and human science make appropriate contributions.

Religious social ethics is a reflective and transformative

process. Its role in society is to bring forth possibilities for public decision and responsibility. In this sense, it is a discipline of freedom, committed to the enhancement of human powers to shape the future in the light of its legacy of symbols and in the context of social struggles. Religious social ethics has the task and privilege of opening the horizon of possibilities in a people's struggle for justice and peace. These open horizons disclose possibilities of commitment and action. At this threshold, only a people can decide whether to continue in complicity with injustice or to begin resistance (Sölle).

NOTES

1. Madathilparampil Mamman Thomas is a major figure in the ecumenical movement. His visit at Princeton Theological Seminary opened many vistas of reflection for faculty and students.
2. Roger Hutchinson of the University of Toronto drew the author into reflection on this very important inquiry and much that follows is indebted to his work and insight.
3. Professor Louis Rousseau of the University of Québec at Montréal suggested this area of inquiry to the author.
4. Martin Heidegger developed the thesis that the drive to mastery arose from the metaphysical ground of classical philosophy which found a place in medieval theology (Heidegger, 1977). Alternative theories locate the techno-society within the emergence of industrial capitalism, but by the nineteenth century the two movements are inseparable.
5. Bishop Remi J. De Roo, president of the Social Affairs Department of the Canadian Catholic Conference of Bishops, outlined this domination by corporate interests in the United States in a memorandum of April 14, 1977, referring to several studies: *Foreign Ownership and the Structure of Canadian Industry* (Ottawa: Queen's Printer, 1968) and *The Gray Report* (Ottawa: Queen's Printer, 1973).
6. The research on this problem has been done by the Center for Suicide Research, Veterans Administration, Wadsworth Medical Center, Los Angeles, California; see Report No. 4, January 1978, and subsequent releases.

WORKS CITED

BANFIELD, EDWARD, 1974, *The Unheavenly City Revisited.* Boston: Little, Brown.

BARFIELD, OWEN, 1965, *Saving the Appearances.* New York: Harcourt, Brace and World, Inc.

BARKER, ERNEST, 1959, *The Political Thought of Plato and Aristotle.* New York: Dover Publications, Inc.

BARNET, RICHARD, 1980, *The Lean Years.* New York: Simon and Schuster.

BAUM, GREGORY, 1975, *Religion and Alienation.* New York: Paulist Press.

BERGER, PETER L., AND LUCKMANN, THOMAS, 1966, *The Social Construction of Reality.* Garden City, NY: Doubleday & Company.

BERGER, THOMAS H., 1977, *Northern Frontier, Northern Homeland: The Report of the MacKenzie Valley Pipeline Inquiry.* 2 vols.

———, 1980, "Science and Technology as Power." In *Faith and Science in an Unjust World.* Vol. 1. Ed. Roger L. Shinn. Philadelphia: Fortress Press.

BLUNT, ANTHONY, 1975, *Artistic Theory in Italy, 1450–1600.* New York: Oxford University Press.

BOHANNAN, PAUL, 1980, "Culture by Numbers." *Science 80* (Sept./Oct.): 28–30.

BUBER, MARTIN, 1952, *The Eclipse of God.* New York: Harper and Row, Harper Torchbooks.

———, 1958, *Hasidism and Modern Man.* New York: Harper and Row, Harper Torchbooks.

CAMUS, ALBERT, 1955, *The Myth of Sisyphus and Other Essays.* New York: Vintage Books.

CASSIRER, ERNST, 1951, *The Philosophy of the Enlightenment.* Princeton, NJ: Princeton University Press.

CONE, JAMES H., 1970, *A Black Theology of Liberation*. New York: J. B. Lippincott Co.

CORNFORD, FRANCIS MACDONALD, 1937, *Plato's Cosmology*. New York: Bobbs-Merrill Co.

DAVIS, CHARLES, 1980, *Theology and Political Society*. Cambridge: Cambridge University Press.

DEBELL, GARETT, ed., 1970. *The Environmental Handbook*. New York: Ballantine Books Inc.

DELORIA, VINE, JR., 1973, *God Is Red*. New York: Grosset and Dunlap.

DEWEY, JOHN, 1954, *Art as Experience*. New York: G. P. Putnam and Sons, Capricorn Books.

DIXON, JOHN, 1978, *Art and the Theological Imagination*. New York: Seabury Press.

DURKA, GLORIA, AND SMITH, JOANMARIE, 1979, *Aesthetic Dimensions of Religious Education*. New York: Paulist Press.

ELIADE, MIRCEA, 1954, *The Myth of the Eternal Return*. New York: Bollingen Foundation.

———, 1958, *Patterns in Comparative Religions*. New York: Sheed and Ward.

———, 1959, *The Sacred and the Profane: The Nature of Religion*. New York: Harcourt, Brace and World, Inc.

EMMET, DOROTHY, 1966, *Rules, Roles and Relations*. New York: St. Martin's Press.

ERIKSON, ERIK, 1964, *Insight and Responsibility*. New York: W. W. Norton.

FALLERS, LLOYD, 1973, *Inequality: Social Stratification Reconsidered*. Chicago: University of Chicago Press.

FALWELL, JERRY, 1981, "Penthouse Interview: Reverend Jerry Falwell." *Penthouse Magazine,* March 1981.

FARLEY, EDWARD, 1975, *Ecclesial Man: A Social Phenomenology of Faith and Reality*. Philadelphia: Fortress Press.

FIERRO, ALFREDO, 1977, *The Militant Gospel: A Critical Introduction to Political Theologies*. Maryknoll, NY: Orbis Books.

FRANKFORT, H. AND H. A., WILSON, JOHN A., JACOBSEN, THORKILD, AND IRWIN, W. A., 1946, *The Intellectual Adventure of Ancient Man: An Essay on Speculative Thought in the Middle East*. Chicago: University of Chicago Press.

FREUD, SIGMUND, 1953, *The Interpretation of Dreams, Standard Edition,* Vols. 4 and 5. Ed. James L. Strachey. London: Hogarth Press.

FRIEDMAN, MILTON, 1962, *Capitalism and Freedom*. Chicago: University of Chicago Press.

GADAMER, HANS-GEORGE, 1975, *Truth and Method*. London: Sheed and Ward.

GAMBLE, D. J., 1978, "The Berger Inquiry: An Impact Assessment Process." *Science* 199: 946–51.

GARFINKEL, HAROLD, 1967, *Studies in Ethnomethodology*. Englewood Cliffs, NJ: Prentice-Hall.

GEERTZ, CLIFFORD, 1973, *The Interpretation of Cultures*. New York: Basic Books, Inc.

GOFFMAN, ERVING, 1961, *Asylums: Essay on the Social Situation of Mental Patients and Other Inmates*. New York: Doubleday and Co., Anchor Books.

GORDON, DAVID, 1977, *Problems in Political Economy*. Toronto: C. D. Heath and Co.

GOTTWALD, NORMAN, 1979, *The Tribes of Jahweh*. Maryknoll, NY: Orbis Books.

GOULDNER, ALVIN W., 1976, *The Dialectic of Ideology and Technology*. New York: Seabury Press.

GUTIERREZ, GUSTAVO, 1973, *A Theology of Liberation: History, Politics and Salvation*. Maryknoll, NY: Orbis Books.

HEIDEGGER, MARTIN, 1962, *Being and Time*. Trans. John Macquarrie and Edward Robinson. London: SCM Press, Ltd.

———, 1971, *Poetry, Language, Thought*. Trans. Albert Hofstadter. New York: Harper and Row.

———, 1972, *On Time and Being*. Trans. Joan Stambaugh. New York: Harper and Row.

———, 1973, *The End of Philosophy*. Trans. Joan Stambaugh. New York: Harper and Row.

———, 1977, *The Question Concerning Technology and Other Essays*. Trans. William Lovitt. New York: Harper and Brothers, Colophon Books.

———, 1979, *Nietzsche, Volume I: The Will to Power as Art*. Trans. David F. Krell. New York: Harper and Row.

HESCHEL, ABRAHAM J., 1962, *The Prophets*. New York: The Jewish Publication Society of America.

HORNEY, KAREN, 1937, *The Neurotic Personality of Our Time*. New York: W. W. Norton and Co.

HUIZINGA, JOHAN, 1955, *Homo Ludens*. Boston: Beacon Press.

HUSSERL, EDMUND, 1960, *Cartesian Meditations: An Introduction to Phenomenology*. The Hague: Martinus Nijhoff.

HUTCHINSON, ROGER, 1980, "Native Peoples in a Technological Society: The Struggle for Self-Determination." Paper delivered at the International Association for the History of Religions. Winnipeg, Canada. August 1980.

HUTCHINSON, ROGER, AND WINTER, GIBSON, 1981, "Citizens, Experts and Public Policy: Canadian Churches and the Mackenzie Valley Pipeline Inquiry." Paper delivered at the American Association for the Advancement of Science. Toronto, Canada. January 8, 1981.

JUNG, CARL GUSTAV, 1958, *Psyche and Symbol: A Selection from the Writings of C. G. Jung*. Ed. Violet S. de Laszlo. Garden City, NY: Doubleday and Co., Anchor Books.

KENICK, HELEN A., 1979, "Toward a Biblical Basis for Creation Theology." In *Western Spirituality*. Ed. Matthew Fox. Notre Dame, IN: Fides/Claretian.

KLEE, PAUL, 1961, *The Thinking Eye: Paul Klee Notebooks*. Vol. 1. Ed. Jurg Spiller. New York: George Wittenborn.

———, 1970, *The Nature of Nature: Paul Klee Notebooks*. Vol. 2, Ed. Heinz Norden. New York: George Wittenborn.

KOHUT, H., 1971, *The Analysis of the Self*. New York: International University Press.

LAMB, MATTHEW, 1975, "The Theory-Praxis Relationship in Contemporary Christian Theologies." *Proceedings of Catholic Theological Society of America*. Vols. 30–31 (1975–76): 149–78.

LASCH, CHRISTOPHER, 1978, *The Culture of Narcissism*. New York: Norton.

MACPHERSON, C. B., 1962, *The Political Theory of Possessive Individualism*. New York: Oxford University Press.

MALINOWSKI, BRONISLAW, 1932, *Argonauts of the Pacific*. London: George Routledge & Sons, Ltd.

MANNHEIM, KARL, 1936, *Ideology and Utopia*. Trans. Louis Wirth and Edward Shils. New York: Harcourt, Brace and Co.

MARX, KARL, 1938, *The German Ideology*. Pts. 1 and 3, with F. Engels. Ed. with an Introduction by R. Pascal. London: Lawrence and Wishart.

———, 1970, *Critique of Hegel's Philosophy of Right*. Ed. Joseph O'Malley. Cambridge: The University Press.

MCCULLUM, HUGH, AND KARMEL MCCULLUM, 1975, *This Land Is Not for Sale: Canada's Original People and Their Land: A Saga of Neglect, Exploitation and Conflict*. Toronto, Canada: Anglican Book Centre.

MIGLIORE, DANIEL, 1980, *Call to Freedom: Liberation Theology and the Future of Christian Doctrine*. Philadelphia: Westminster Press.

MOL, HANS J., 1976, *Identity and the Sacred: A Sketch for a New Social-Scientific Theory of Religion*. Agincourt, Canada: The Book Society of Canada Limited.

MOYNIHAN, DANIEL, 1965, *The Negro Family: The Case for National Action*. Washington, D.C.: U.S. Department of Labor, U.S. Government Printing Office.

MUMFORD, LEWIS, 1970, *The Myth of the Machine, Part Two: The Pentagon of Power*. New York: Harcourt Brace Jovanovich, A Harvest Book.

MYRDAL, GUNNAR, 1944, *An American Dilemma: The Negro Problem and Modern Democracy*. With assistance of Richard Sterner and Arnold Rose. New York: Harper and Brothers.

NATIONAL COMMISSION ON NEIGHBORHOODS, 1979, *People, Building Neighborhoods*. Final Report to the President and the Congress of the U.S. Washington, D.C.: U.S. Government Printing Office.

NISBET, ROBERT A., 1969, *Social Change and History*. New York: Oxford University Press.

OGLETREE, THOMAS W., 1980, "The Activity of Interpreting in Moral Judgment." *Journal of Religious Ethics* 8: 1–26.

PARSONS, TALCOTT, AND CLARK, KENNETH, eds., 1965–66, *The Negro American. Daedalus*, Fall 1965, Spring 1966.

PEPPER, STEPHEN, 1961, *World Hypotheses*. Berkeley: University of California Press.

PERCY, WALKER, 1979, *The Message in the Bottle*. New York: Farrar, Strauss and Giroux.

PICKERING, GEORGE, 1978, "The Task of Social Ethics." In *Belief and Ethics*. Ed. Widick Schroeder and Gibson Winter. Chicago: Center for the Scientific Study of Religion.

PITCHER, ALVIN, AND WINTER, GIBSON, 1977, "Perspectives in Religious Social Ethics." *Journal of Religious Ethics* 5: 68–89.

RASCHKE, CARL, 1978, "The End of Theology." *Journal of the American Academy of Religion* 46: 159–79.

RICOEUR, PAUL, 1967, *Husserl: An Analysis of His Phenomenology*. Trans. Edward G. Ballard and Lester E. Embree. Evanston, IL: Northwestern University Press.

———, 1974, *The Conflict of Interpretations*. Evanston, IL: Northwestern University Press.

———, 1976, *Interpretation Theory: Discourse and the Surplus of Meaning*. Fort Worth, TX: Texas Christian University Press.

———, 1978, *The Philosophy of Paul Ricoeur: An Anthology of His Work*. Ed. Charles E. Reagan and David Stewart. Boston: Beacon Press.

———, 1980, *Essays on Biblical Interpretation*. Ed. Lewis S. Mudge. Philadelphia: Fortress Press.

ROSZAK, THEODORE, 1973, *Where the Wasteland Ends*. Garden City, NY: Doubleday and Co., Anchor Books.

RUETHER, ROSEMARY R., 1975, *New Woman, New Earth: Sexist Ideologies and Human Liberation*. New York: Seabury Press.

RYAN, WILLIAM, 1976, *Blaming the Victim*. New York: Random House, Vintage Books.

SARTRE, JEAN-PAUL, 1956, *Being and Nothingness*. Trans. Hazel E. Barnes. New York: Philosophical Library.

SCHUTZ, ALFRED, 1962, *Collected Papers I: The Problem of Social Reality*. The Hague: Martinus Nijhoff.

———, 1964, *Collected Papers II: Studies in Social Theory*. The Hague: Martinus Nijhoff.

———, 1971, *Collected Papers III: Studies in Phenomenological Philosophy*. The Hague: Martinus Nijhoff.

SEGUNDO, JUAN LUIS, 1976, *The Liberation of Theology*. Trans. John Drury. Maryknoll, NY: Orbis Books.

SENNETT, RICHARD, 1977, *The Fall of Public Man: On the Social Psychology of Capitalism*. New York: Random House, Vintage Books.

SEWELL, ELIZABETH, 1964, *The Human Metaphor*. Notre Dame, IN: University of Notre Dame Press.

SLATER, PETER, 1978, *The Dynamics of Religion*. New York: Harper and Row.

SMITH, LILLIAN, 1949, *Killers of the Dream*. New York: Norton.

SÖLLE, DOROTHEE, 1974, *Political Theology*. Trans. John Shelley. Philadelphia: Fortress Press.

SPENCER, THEODORE, 1942, *Shakespeare and the Nature of Man*. New York: Macmillan Co.

SPRING, DAVID, AND SPRING, EILEEN, eds., 1974, *Ecology and Religion in History*. New York: Harper and Row, Harper Torchbooks.

STABLER, J. C., AND OLFERT, M. R., 1980, "Gaslight Follies: The Political Economy of the Western Arctic." *Canadian Public Policy* 6: 374–88

STRAUSS, ANSELM L., 1959, *Mirrors and Masks, The Search for Identity*. Glencoe, IL: Free Press.

TROELTSCH, ERNST, 1949, *The Social Teachings of the Christian Churches*. Vol. 1. New York: Macmillan Co.

VANSTONE, JAMES W., 1962, *Athapaskan Adaptations: Hunters and Fishermen of the Subarctic Forests*. Chicago: Aldine Publishing Co.

WARNOCK, MARY, 1976, *Imagination*. Berkeley: University of California Press.

WATKINS, MEL, ed., 1977, *Dene Nation: The Colony Within*. Toronto, Canada: Toronto University Press.

WEBER, MAX, 1949, *Max Weber on the Methodology of the Social Sciences*. Ed. Edward A. Shils and Henry A. Finch. Glencoe, IL: Free Press.

———, 1958, *The Protestant Ethic and the Spirit of Capitalism*. Trans. Talcott Parsons. New York: Scribner.

WHEELWRIGHT, PHILIP, 1962, *Metaphor and Reality*. Bloomington, IN: University of Indiana Press.

———, 1968, *The Burning Fountain*. Bloomington, IN: University of Indiana Press.

WINTER, GIBSON, 1963, "Society and Morality in the French Tradition." *Review of Religious Research* 5: 11–21.

———, 1966, *Elements for a Social Ethic*. New York: The Macmillan Co.

———, 1979, "A Proposal for a Political Ethic." *Review of Religious Research* 21: 87–107.

YANKELOVICH, DANIEL, AND BARRETT, WILLIAM, 1970, *Ego and Instinct: The Psychoanalytic View of Human Nature—Revised*. New York: Random House, Vintage Books.

INDEX